Contents

REMEMBER SCARBOROUGH

A RESULT OF THE FIRST ARMS RACE OF THE TWENTIETH CENTURY

BOB CLARKE

AMBERLEY

For the Professionals
Brian Hopkins, Mick Aston and Julian Richards
You are all equally responsible for sowing the seed!

First published 2010

Amberley Publishing Plc
Cirencester Road, Chalford,
Stroud, Gloucestershire, GL6 8PE

www.amberleybooks.com

British Library Cataloguing in Publication Data.
A catalogue record for this book is available from the British Library.

ISBN 978 1 84868 111 8

Typesetting and Origination by Amberley Publishing.
Printed in Great Britain.

Acknowledgements

The customary acknowledgements don't really apply here. I have undertaken this work as independently as possible, as I wanted to draw my own conclusions. The only way to achieve that was to start from scratch, and I feel it's been worth it. I'm sure some will read this and comment that I've missed out 'this' or forgotten to include 'that'. This is inevitable. To them, using the concept of 'last word theory', I say, 'Include these in your own account.'

Some thanks are due. Sarah, who has only just got to grips with archaeology and aviation, now has to contend with ships as well. Also, many of my colleagues who are ex-Royal Navy and have had great fun sorting out my lack of nautical terminology; Phil Harris features largely here. Mark Marsay should also be mentioned; his Herculean effort chronicling the Bombardment of Scarborough will not be surpassed. However, the biggest thanks are indeed due to Campbell and all those at Amberley who have been expecting this work for what must have seemed an eternity!

Preface

The study of history is a subjective occupation. All too often, the researcher encounters, or has to rely on, material of a second- or third-hand nature. Subsequently, this is usually biased, especially when linked to national interests or written by the pen of the victor, as is the case with so much of history. The teaching of history in secondary education is especially, in my view, restricted by those very same traits. It is not uncommon to encounter adults who have suffered at the hands of a poor history curriculum. However, speak to anyone who has been out of mainstream education for a decade or so, and you soon discover they find one historical period or another interesting. From the armchair archaeologist to the bar room general, everyone has their opinion or can discuss this event or that anniversary. So why is this?

Well, two things really. Firstly, what makes a difference, I think, is a teacher, lecturer or presenter's ability to breathe life into a period, making it relevant to the student. This is where I turn to my experience of history in the mid-1970s and my secondary school history teacher Mr Hopkins. The syllabus at that time concerned itself with the French and Agricultural Revolution, two mutually exclusive, and, for boys aged thirteen and fourteen, bloody boring subjects! So thank goodness for Mr Hopkins. He had that enviable knack of noticing when the class had had enough and immediately spicing it up with such comments as 'When the Germans came to town' and 'Did I tell you about the Beaker Folk?' From then on, the class would hang on his every word. A true historian and one that has had a considerable influence on my life ever since.

One only has to look at the calendar to realise the reasons behind including the 'old enemy' in the syllabus. The Heath Government had taken Britain into the Common Market a couple of years earlier, and there was still discussion over whether we were just playing 'second fiddle' to the French. Clearly, in educational terms, that was the case. A suggestion of political interference in the history curriculum is probably raising the reader's eyebrow about now, however, any type of 'national' curriculum is naturally susceptible. When I taught adult students GCSE Archaeology throughout the 1990s, I was surprised to learn that an act of invasion should be classed as 'migration' wherever possible – I'm not sure Harold would have agreed with that – and that Roman coinage should be promoted as Europe's first truly international currency – no direction in the form of the Euro there then! Enough. Back to Scarborough in the 1970s. It was the Beaker Folk, who we learned lived on Castle Hill, that really caught my imagination. So much so that when I stared down at the face of several during an excavation at Boscombe Down a few years ago, I could not help wondering what Mr Hopkins would have made of it all. So it turns out it's not what you are taught in your formative years in this business but how the seeds are sown; for me, that was the Beakers and Scarborough generally.

That brings me to my second point. Churchill once helpfully pointed out, 'History will be kind to me for I intend to write it.' And write it he did, along with a vast number of other quotable statements and phrases. One, the 'Iron Curtain', made in his now-famous Fulton University speech, and its forty-year aftermath, has defined my recent career, especially through the last few books I have written. However, we should be mindful that, whilst many people write history, nobody really has the last word. For the last ten years or so, I have spoken at many institutions, engaging audiences with stories of Prehistory, Saxon executions and postwar Britain. Most of the material has been new, relying little on the work of others, save for the odd illustration or quotation; however, even my originality does not ensure I enjoy the last word – that becomes immediately clear once the chair asks for questions.

So, with Mr Hopkins in mind, onto this book. As to having the last word, well I am sure this will not be the final work about the Bombardment of Scarborough or the arms race that led up to it. However, I do intend it to be close. Applying the 'last word' principle, in 1999, Mark Marsay published a definitive account of 16 December 1914 and the unfolding events on that morning, capturing the last few surviving eyewitness accounts and recording much that was then available. Luckily, 16 December was his focus; I, however, like to place events in context wherever possible, as this is the only sure way to understanding them. I am not convinced the raids on the East Coast were intended to be as flagrant an attack on defenceless women and children as the contemporary press or later accounts have suggested. I should point out here that I in no way condone such actions, however, if we are to understand fully why 16 December 1914 became such an infamous date in the town's, and indeed Britain's, calendar, then we must place it in context. Further, previously unexplored documents must be considered and, even more importantly, an open mind kept. Consequently, this work takes us around the world and through a series of treaties; treaties the signatories hoped would never be honoured. It recounts the first arms race of the twentieth century, dictating this is not just a history of the bombardment of the East Coast; moreover, it chronicles the destruction of social and political innocence.

A word on the book's layout is required here. I decided early in the production of this work that the events in Scarborough would be the focus of the bombardment section, as this was, by far, the most contentious part of the whole raid. It is impossible to talk of Scarborough without mentioning Whitby and Hartlepool, but all three towns' stories have been well trodden, and it was not my intention to reproduce that work. Therefore, for that reason, Scarborough features more than the other two towns. It also seemed logical to use many of the photographs taken immediately after the event to illustrate the bombardment of the East Coast; subsequently, they form a major part of the initial chapter.

Scarborough before the storm *c.* 1906. It's a sobering thought that many of the boys on this photograph would have fought in the First World War. Who knows how many returned?

Further underscoring the 'last word' principle, in 1915, Frederick Miller wrote in his foreword,

> All the naval facts connected with it cannot be known for some time, but it is essential to the future historian of the stupendous events of this period that he should have all that tragic forty-minute meaning at his command. For him, for the inhabitants of these stricken towns, for their relatives and friends at home and abroad this little book is written.

Under Shell-Fire
Frederick Miller
West Hartlepool
January 1915

I fully echo those words; every modern historian should strive to build a springboard of knowledge that will propel those who come after to greater understanding. I hope you consider this work that springboard.

Diagram published in the *Scarborough Evening News* after the raid.

One

'Scintillating Scarborough: They refer to Scarborough of last Tuesday, not today'

In the 17 December 1914 edition of *The New York Times*, Ruth Kauffman recounted the following eyewitness account:

> Cloughton, Scarborough England Dec. 17. – It's a very curious thing to watch a bombardment from your house. Everybody knew the Kaiser would do it. But there was a little doubt about the date, and then somehow the spy hunting sport took up general attention. When the Kaiser did send his card here yesterday morning it was quite as much of a surprise as most Christmas cards – from a forgotten friend.
>
> Eighteen people were killed yesterday morning between 8 o'clock and 8.30 in the streets and houses of Scarborough by German shrapnel, 200 were wounded, and more than 200 houses were damaged or demolished.

Ruth Kauffman was the wife of American journalist Reginald Wright Kauffman. Both were prolific authors who through the 1920s turned their work increasingly to matters surrounding socialism. Cloughton, situated a few miles north of Scarborough, has a commanding panorama of the coast, granting the Kauffmans a grandstand view of the morning's events. Naturally, as reporters, it was deemed necessary to make a trip into town at the earliest opportunity.

> We drove to Scarborough. We had not gone one mile of the distance when we began to meet people coming in the opposite direction. A small white-faced boy in a milk cart that early every morning makes its Scarborough rounds, showed us a piece of shell he had picked up and said it had first struck a man a few yards from him and killed the man. A woman carrying a basket told us, with trembling lips, that men and women were lying about the streets dead. The postman assured us that Scarborough was in flames. A road worker told us we should be turned back and another man warned us to beware of a big hole in the road further along, large enough to swallow our horse and trap; yet we could certainly see no flames issuing from Scarborough, which now lay directly before us.

It is worth considering the words of Kauffman's report as you follow, through this initial section, the events of 16 December 1914, as they illustrate how one person's experience is never quite the same as another's. Often, as was the case in the aftermath of Scarborough, conflicting reports were published for an international audience, with scant regard for accuracy. The aftermath is dealt with at the other end of this work; here, we investigate as best as possible the bombardments effects on Scarborough.

A little after eight o'clock (nine o'clock Standard European time), SMS *von der Tann* leading SMS *Derfflinger* steamed southerly past the castle headland, referred to in German accounts as 'Scarborough Rock'. The ships had closed to around one nautical mile from the coastline off Robin Hood's Bay before turning south, following a parallel course with the morning train along the Whitby–Scarborough North Eastern Railway's coastal line en route to the town. A short five minutes later, both ships opened up with broadsides, *Derfflinger* on the castle, *von der Tann* into the town.

The castle had seen its fair share of action over the years, two extremely costly sieges during the Civil War that had led to the keep being partially destroyed and the walls slighted thereafter. In 1745-46, a barracks had been built into the south curtain wall in response to the final Jacobite Rebellion. At this time, defensive batteries were also built, one facing north and a further two southward over the town and harbour. By 1900, the castle had long since lost any true military significance, presiding instead over the rapid growth of the town into one of Europe's foremost spa locations and the destination of many a factory fortnight holiday. Indeed, the barracks had not seen regular military occupation since 1878; they were not destined to again, as the roof and north-facing wall was blown out by German shells.

The keep was struck twice, the walls were breached in a number of places, and a small wireless station built some time earlier was also damaged beyond repair. The Master Gunner's House, situated close to the keep, was also badly damaged. It had been built in 1748 as living accommodation for the Master and had been partially occupied until the turn of the century. The area between the old town and south curtain wall, known locally as 'the dykes', was also ploughed up by a number of shells.

Damage to the town was far more extensive than that inflicted on the castle. The Grand Hotel, one of Scarborough's most recognisable landmarks, received over thirty hits from shells of various sizes. The hotel, an imposing structure financed in 1867 by Scarborough businessmen, indeed the biggest brick-built structure in Europe on completion, suffered £13,000 worth of damage. Attic accommodation frequented by staff, sea-view suites, the restaurant and annex containing the picture house on the Foreshore were all badly affected. When *The New York Times* ran a photographic supplement on the bombardment on Sunday 3 January 1915, the wreckage of the Grand Restaurant featured as a half-page headline image in the broadsheet. Luckily, only a handful of guests were in residence due to the time of year; had it been earlier in the season, the Grand Restaurant would have been full of people taking breakfast about the time of the bombardment. Properties around the Grand were also damaged, including the Spa Boarding House on St Nicholas Parade owned by Mr Ashley.

The Grand was not the only hotel to be hit. The Royal Hotel, Carlton, George, Granville, Pavilion, Prince of Wales, Balmoral, numerous guest houses and at least

SCARBOROUGH BOMBARDED BY THE GERMANS. DECEMBER 1914.

Above left: The bombardment begins. Artists often re-touched or spiced up images, especially those for public consumption.

Above right: The bombardment of Scarborough by German warships. Note the castle headland. A print by Willy Stöwer sold in Germany to provide for naval veterans.

Slighting the castle walls.

The old barracks on the castle.

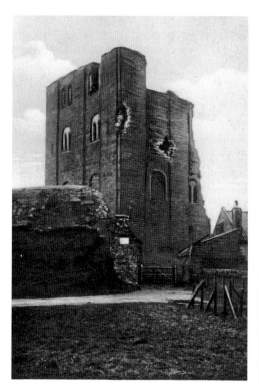

Above left: The keep now with some modern battle scars.

Above right: The speak your weight machine blown out of the Grand Hotel.

three temperance establishments all suffered varying degrees of damage. The Royal Hotel was hit, possibly by a ricochet off the corner of the Town Hall, the shell piercing the building and destroying the Royal Suite as well as breaking 160 panes of glass. The Prince of Wales was severely damaged by a shell exploding in the street, shrapnel scarring much of the frontage that had to be replaced at a cost of £4,000.

Indeed, the Esplanade area received several hits, damaging a high number of properties and killing the first two of nineteen people in the process. The chemist's shop of Clare & Hunts on the corner of South Street was partially demolished when a shell exploded close by; unfortunately, Leonard Ellis, the shop's porter, became the first victim of the bombardment, as he was caught in the blast. Seconds later, another shell exploded in the road, killing driver Harry Frith. Further properties on South Street were wrecked, including the antiques shop owned and run by Charles Smith, damaged by the shell that killed Mr Frith. Next door to the chemist's, another shell caused structural damage to a branch of the London & Joint Stock Bank.

Scarborough's Liberal Member of Parliament, Walter Rea, was not immune; his house received extensive damage when a shell passed through a second-floor window, detonating inside the house. Luckily, three occupants – Rea was actually in London at the time – escaped major injury. A hundred yards further north, a shell destroyed the third floor of No. 6 Belvoir Terrace, demolishing part of the roof and balcony and trapping the occupant, Mrs Keble, inside. More shells damaged the vicarage and a house in Somerset Terrace. Just behind this area lay the main railway station; clearly the houses in the Crescent area fell victim to shells intended to hit the station and line to York – none did.

Not all houses in the town were as substantially built as the ones in the area of Wood End and the Crescent. Scarborough had been, over the last 100 years, steadily expanding as more people moved into the town to cater for the holiday trade; subsequently, large areas contained close-knit, brick-built terraced housing. When high-explosive shells began to fall in those areas, the damage was so great a number of structures were subsequently demolished or practically rebuilt from scratch. It was a simple terraced house that became the scene of the largest tragedy and gave rise to the recruitment drive slogan 'Avenge the Baby Killers of Scarborough'. Number 2 Wykeham Street was home to the Bennett family, and as was often the case at the turn of the century, a number of 'paying guests'. An eyewitness, Mrs Annie Agar, who lived across the road at No. 1, watched the shell strike.

> I was standing at the corner of St Johns Road and saw it all. The shell came flying straight over the railway bridge – it smashed a lot of windows in Gladstone Road School – and went clean through Mrs Bennett's house. The place was blown up and things went flying in all directions.

The blast was such that the whole front of the house was demolished with every room in the house wrecked. The majority of the family had been in the kitchen, close to where the shell detonated, and subsequently suffered the full force of the blast. Christopher, the Bennett's twenty-five-year-old son, later recounted the explosion.

The Saloon Bar of the Grand Hotel.

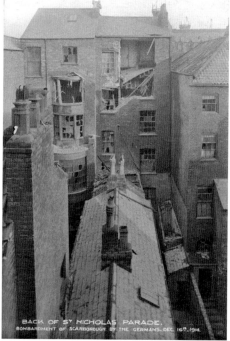

Above left: A seaward-facing room in the Grand Hotel.

Above right: St Nicholas Parade.

Above left: The Royal Hotel was probably damaged by a ricochet off the Town Hall.

Above right: The seaward-facing corner of the Town Hall.

The hole at the Prince of Wales Hotel became a standard feature in photographs.

Above left: The Chemists on the corner of South Street.

Above right: Charles Smith's antiques shop on South Street. Smith is holding up a piece of shrapnel.

The London & Joint Stock Bank.

Above left: Scarborough's MP Walter Rea's house in the Crescent.

Above right: No. 6 Belvoir Terrace.

Above left: Wykeham Street, the scene of four deaths.

Above right: Inside No. 2 Wykeham Street.

GERMAN RAID DEC.16TH 1914, HOUSE IN WYKEHAM ST. SCARBOROUGH.   4 KILLED.

Wykeham Street.

Father and Mother and the two children were in the kitchen and Father called out to me 'Come on lad, let's away downstairs. It's the Germans. Come and look after mother.' But before I had time to get downstairs it had all happened. The shell hit the house fully and I fell through the bedroom floor into the kitchen. It was a long time before I realised where I was. I was practically buried in stuff. When at last I could look around me, I had only a shirt and one slipper on.

The four fatalities, Mrs Johanna Bennett (fifty-eight), Albert Bennett (twenty-two) a Territorial driver with the Royal Field Artillery, John Ward (ten) and George James Barnes (five), all suffered terrible shrapnel wounds. Albert Bennett, who had been tending the fire at the time, was described as being 'riddled with shot'; he died in hospital. Mrs Bennett and the two children died soon after the explosion. Remarkably, Mrs Edmonds (ninety), the Bennett's lodger and an invalid of two years, survived, literally walking away from the rubble, much to everyone's surprise.

Wykeham Street was not the only private dwelling damaged; across town, shells were demolishing more and more houses as the German cruisers aimed for geographically obscured targets. In Commercial Street, No. 79 took the full force of an exploding shell, totally wrecking the interior and leaving the whole frontage in danger of collapse. Later in the afternoon, it was discovered that two of the occupants were still in the house; one, fifty-five-year-old Jane White, suffered injuries requiring hospitalisation. The blast also affected the home of William Webster next door, and two further houses in the street received damage as more shells fell in the area. The wife of the proprietor of Merryweather's food store was killed as she helped people to cover. Her husband was buried in the rubble but survived the ordeal.

A number of properties on North Marine Road were damaged as the ships shelled the areas of town directly behind and to the north of the castle. As the road runs parallel with the cliff top, it is reasonable to assume one cruiser caused the damage. Chimneys were knocked from two houses, whilst at No. 164 and No. 166, the shells found their mark, destroying the upper two floors. No one was injured, but when postman Mr Southwick returned from his round, he discovered his house devastated. He later posed in the ruin of the house for photographers.

Victoria Road saw a number of hits along its entire length. Running south-west from the old town, behind it lay the substantial goods yards of the railway. As the road serviced a large number of the terraced streets, it had become one of the main shopping thoroughfares, many road-facing properties were businesses; luckily, it was too early in the morning for any to be full. It was a number of days before the area could be declared safe; as reports suggest, not a pane of glass was left intact along the whole length of the road.

'Victoria Road Havoc,' reported the *Scarborough Evening News*. 'Turning the corner into Victoria Road the observer found only too effective evidence of the enemy's fire. Hardly any house escaped. On both sides of the road great cavities indicate the tremendous quantity of glass which must have been smashed. Shops and residences suffered alike, and damage was done to many tradesmen's stock.'

In the South Cliff area a wide variety of structures were damaged as the German vessels raked the Esplanade area, a clearly visible feature of Scarborough. A semi-detached house, No. 14 Lonsdale Road, thankfully unoccupied at the time, had the top two floors blown into the street. In the same salvo, maid Edith Crosby died when

Above left: No. 79 Commercial Street.

Above right: Merryweather's food store on Prospect Road. The shopkeeper (in the apron) lost his wife in the explosion.

Postman Southwick poses in the remains of his front room.

The upstairs bedroom of 118 Victoria Road; many shops and houses were damaged in this area.

a shell that failed to explode passed through the property she worked in and then out into the garden. A further clutch of shells, again probably one salvo, dropped on and around the house of former County Sheriff John Turner. The first of three to hit the large house, Dunollie, demolished two of the eight substantial pillars that held up the front of the structure, blasting masonry far and wide. Postman Alfred Beal is thought to have reached the front steps of the building as the shell detonated. He was killed instantly, his body blown back down the drive by the full force of the 16-inch shell exploding in front of him. A further shell entered the house and wrecked the library, killing maid Margret Briggs, whilst a third narrowly missed the owner, causing more damage to Dunollie's interior.

A single shell penetrated the roof of All Saints church on Falsgrave Road, presumably intended to hit the excursion railway station close by. The church was one of several places of worship damaged by shell fire, including St Mary's, St Martin's on the Hill, St Peter's, St Saviour's and the Primitive Methodists chapel on Castle Road.

Above left: No. 14 Lonsdale Road. This was empty. The house next door had visitors; they escaped injury.

Above right: Dunollie. The postman Alfred Beal's body was blown back down the drive by the force of the blast. The maid also died here.

Above left: All Saints church, Falsgrave Road. One of several places of worship damaged that day.

Above right: The final shot passed straight through the tower of the lighthouse before hitting the Grand Hotel.

The lighthouse tower was removed in early 1915 and the place was rebuilt after the war.

Casualties being driven to hospital on makeshift transport.

Kolberg fights rough sea off the coast of Scarborough whilst laying mines. Scarborough Castle can be seen on the right.

The mines left claimed a number of victims over the coming months.

The final shot of the bombardment passed clean through the tower of the lighthouse, wrecking the harbour-master's bedroom and causing his wife to run for cover behind the leeward harbour wall. The power of the shell passing through the lighthouse blew all the windows out around the lamp before it carried on across the South Bay and hit the Grand Hotel Restaurant, already pretty much damaged beyond repair by then. With that *Derfflinger* and *von der Tann* steamed northward, their next objective the radio station at Whitby. They had left eighteen dead, damage ranged anywhere between blown-out windows to almost destroyed across over 600 buildings and countless injuries to members of the public. The damage to the town had been so extensive because many of the secondary targets were not in the direct line of sight. The railway stations, gasworks, waterworks and more importantly, wireless station at Sandy Bed were all area-shelled. Most of that shot, an estimated 700 shells of various calibre fired in just 23 minutes, landed in residential areas.

Whilst the firing had stopped at Scarborough, the second part of the German operation was still underway. The worsening weather on the trip across the North Sea had meant all but one 'small' cruiser had had to turn back, that '*kleinen Kreuzer*' was the SMS *Kolberg*. Her role was to lay an extended string of 100 mines along the routes local steamer traffic used and to add to the already extensive field off the Humber. The work took 25 minutes, however, was nearly abandoned as the sea swell was so bad the *Kolberg* began to take on water. The operation was a success, as just a few days later, the minesweepers SS *Torquay* and *Night Hawk* were both damaged by mines.

Whitby

With many of the objectives at Scarborough apparently met, *Derfflinger* and *von der Tann* headed north to Whitby, whilst *Kolberg* headed directly for the main rendezvous point. Both ships bombarded the coastal watch station and other wireless-related targets around the harbour area; over two hundred shells were fired in just ten minutes. The first shells struck the cliffs in front of the East Cliff Signal Station, then, getting the range, the gun crews on the *von der Tann* proceeded to demolish the station. The staff evacuated in time with just minor injuries; however, Coastguard Frederick Randall, trying to get a better look at the attacking ships, lost the top of his skull to shrapnel. Admiral Reinhard Scheer later wrote,

> The signalling and coastguard stations at Whitby were destroyed – the second round brought down the signalling flagstaff with the English ensign and the entire station building as well.

Shells dropped all across the Abbey plateau, causing substantial damage to the remains of the eleventh-century monument. The west doorway arch was destroyed and a single shell penetrated the roof of the lodge, the Abbey barn roof was also holed and some windows were damaged in nearby St Mary's church. The majority of shells fired at a secondary wireless station situated in the harbour resulted in major damage to the town. As with Scarborough, fire, although claimed to be directed, looked more like an

Whitby Abbey received damage.

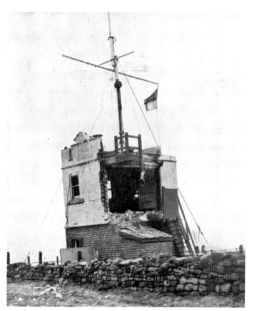 

Above left: The signal station at Whitby was all but destroyed in the attack.

Above right: A boy scout shows the direction from which the shells came that damaged Whitby.

opportunity to 'pepper' the town before making good their escape. The tally at Whitby was nothing like that experienced at Scarborough, around forty properties received damage, three were injured whilst two people died on the day and a further died of their injuries a few days later.

Hartlepool

Whilst SMS *Derfflinger, von der Tann* and *Kolberg* had dealt with the southern part of the operation, three battle cruisers had made their way north. SMS *Seydlitz, Moltke* and *Blücher*, with the commander-in-chief of the whole operation's flag on *Seydlitz*, were to engage the coastal batteries protecting the port and sink as much shipping in the harbour as possible. Four Royal Navy destroyers were patrolling to the north-east of Hartlepool when the lookout reported three large ships running into the coast. It was clear from the range that an attack by torpedoes would be unsuccessful, and so they elected to get in closer. The three German ships had other ideas, and HMS *Doon, Waverley, Moy* and *Test* came under accurate fire almost at once. The destroyers scattered, with *Doon* taking a number of hits. Thinking she was sinking, the Germans broke off – intent on following the original bombardment orders before a major Royal Navy flotilla arrived. In a preset plan, the *Seydlitz* was to engage the Cemetery Battery and local industries, *Moltke* would fire on the Heugh and Lighthouse batteries, whilst *Blücher* would bombard industrial facilities, docks and destroy the gasworks. A bank of fog lying 4,000-5,000 yards offshore helped the three German vessels get close into shore before clear detection, but it had a downside – the bank also dictated the distance from the shore, bringing all within range of the coastal batteries.

Men stationed on the coastal defences had been on alert since 05.30 as London transmitted a 'special warning', advising a sharp lookout to be maintained along the East Coast from dawn. Interestingly, the warning was not to be transmitted widely – a reference to how the information had been obtained. When the four destroyers left Hartlepool around 05.45 to conduct their usual coastal patrol, they too had the 'special warning', and so when the three German ships were encountered, their nationality was immediately recognised. On shore, it was a different matter. Gunners manning the coastal guns could hear the engagement whilst those at the lighthouse battery could see the flashes of fire. Unfortunately, the South Gare Battery had already identified them as British ships flying the White Ensign; to make matters worse, they were of the Indomitable class!

Above: The first shell in Hartlepool struck Cliff Terrace, situated behind the coastal batteries.

Left: The Lighthouse Battery.

'Lets give 'em the works!'

By the time the South Gare Battery realised the 'British' ships were actually firing at Royal Navy destroyers, they had sailed far enough north to be out of range. The Heugh Battery, on hearing the firing, decided it should ready the artillery, just in case. As the ships steamed out from behind the lighthouse (the Heugh Battery's field of view was obscured by the lighthouse – it was demolished soon after the bombardment for this reason), it was clear the White Ensign was in fact the flag of the Imperial German Navy. After a pause, *Seydlitz* fired the first salvo of the Hartlepool bombardment, striking the row of houses directly behind the lighthouse battery and some of the facility. The time was 08.10; the blast killed four soldiers of the 18th Durham Light Infantry – the first to be killed by enemy action on British soil in the First World War.

Now the coastal batteries replied; *Blücher* was struck four times by artillery, putting guns out of action, damaging the optical system and taking down aerials and searchlights. *Seydlitz* took three hits, the shells holing the forward funnel, splintering the engine room and punching a hole below the waterline. Whilst *Moltke* lost a number of cabins as a large-calibre shell struck the foreship. *Moltke* had only been using medium-sized artillery in the bombardment, the heavy being kept in reserve in case the Royal Navy intercepted the action. Once it was recognised the German ships were under threat from coastal fire, the large-calibre weapons were brought to bear. As *Seydlitz* and *Moltke* now took on the bombardment of targets within the town, *Blücher* continued to keep the coastal batteries occupied. Whilst all this was going on, the rest of the coastal patrol, forming part of the 9th Flotilla, were trying to exit Victoria Dock. HMS *Patrol*, *Forward* and the submarine C9, already under sporadic fire, decided to get into open water as soon as possible. The problem was the tide had been going out since early morning; *Patrol* grounded and was struck several times, whilst C9 discovered she had very little to dive in but managed to bump along the bottom. By the time all three vessels had got out of harbour, it was too late – the raiders had headed eastward back into the fog. Military targets, whilst knocked about, had not suffered too badly. No coastal guns were hit or damaged although the facilities were ploughed up in a number of areas. The Durham Light Infantry lost nine men and twelve were wounded; the Royal Navy lost a further nine. The town was a different matter all together.

Damage to Hartlepool was enormous. Shells had dropped in the densely populated areas of the town for over thirty minutes, killing 114 civilians and wounding a further 424. All manner of buildings were damaged, including places of worship, public buildings and many residential properties. One crucial difference between Scarborough and Hartlepool, the one that gave Scarborough the propaganda edge, was the ability of the Hartlepool batteries to fight back. This made the town a legitimate target in prevailing international law. But what were the reasons behind the attacks? For that, we have to turn the clock back to a colonial conflict fifteen years earlier and half a world away.

GIRVAN TERRACE

MANISFORTH TERRACE

RUGBY TERRACE

Top left: No. 7 Victoria Place, Hartlepool.

Top middle: Cleveland Road, Hartlepool.

Top right: The Baptist Chapel, Hartlepool.

Left: Scenes of West Hartlepool after it was shelled by the Germans.

Two

'It was not expenditure that secured efficiency'

On 2 October 1905, a ship was laid down in HM Dockyard Portsmouth that revolutionised naval thinking. She was the Royal Navy's answer to a naval arms race that would end, nine years later, in war. HMS *Dreadnought* became synonymous with battleships from the first half of the twentieth century; however, she was neither the instigator of the arms race, nor was she the only innovation being developed by the world's navies.

HMS *Dreadnought* was the combination of thirty years of technological development coupled with the vision of a forward-looking First Sea Lord. There continues to be discussion as to who was actually responsible for the design, but it is probable that the Italian naval architect Vittorio Cuniberti was first in 1903. Close behind were the British and Americans, both with plans by 1904, but it was the team, led by the First Sea Lord, Admiral Sir John 'Jackie' Fisher, that won out. Fisher's Committee of Designs, which was formed in late 1904, comprised a number of senior figures, including the Director of Naval Construction, Sir Philip Watts. Watts incorporated a new powerplant, the steam turbine, and in so doing greatly increased performance, producing a design that could outrun any other ship at the time of her launch. However, the dreadnought, as the type became known, was the product of war itself, and it is there, in Southern Africa and the Far East, that we have to look to establish the chain of events that eventually led to war with Germany and the bombardment of the East Coast.

The Boer War

The Dutch East India Company founded a settlement at the Cape of Good Hope in 1650 as a link in their trading routes to the East. By the Napoleonic Wars, the Cape had been occupied by the British to safeguard the trading routes to India from French interference. Many Boer (Dutch for farmer) families, resenting British rule, began a major migration into new areas, first along the coast but increasingly north and inland. Known as the Trekboers, the British saw them more as pioneers than exiles, opening up large areas of Southern Africa. Eventually, two states were declared, the Transvaal and Orange Free State, both gaining recognition by the British Government by 1854. That said, from the mid-1830s, relations between the Boer population and local tribes often decayed to a point of conflict.

The discovery of diamonds near the Vaal River in 1867 quickly changed British policy towards the South African interior, effectively removing any chance the Boers had of maintaining any 'isolated' authority. By the mid-1870s, the British had annexed those areas of the Transvaal that were diamond and gold producing. Lord Carnarvon, Colonial Secretary to the Disraeli Government, attempted, in 1875, to broker a deal covering both Boer States, modelling it on the recent organisation of French- and English-speaking Canada; this was rejected, placing both on a path to conflict. The Transvaal was also the focus of territorial demands from the indigenous Zulus led by King Cetshwayo. The King maintained a strong position by courting favour with the British administration in neighbouring Natal whilst modernising his 40,000-strong tribal army with rifles; however, the majority was still armed with shields, spears and clubs.

In 1877, whilst the Boers were still resisting sporadic Zulu attacks, the British annexed the Transvaal, placing the governance of the state under Sir Theophilus Shepstone, Governor of Natal. This quickly shifted the balance of power in the region, as the Zulus now became Britain's adversary in the disputed Transvaal. Pressure was maintained from within by Paul Kruger, who visited London twice to gain assurances that the settlers' homelands would be guaranteed. Kruger was of German descent, his family having migrated to Southern Africa in the eighteenth century. After a distinguished military career, Kruger became vice-president of the Transvaal up to the annexation of the region by the British in 1877. He became the president of the Transvaal in 1880.

Unfortunately, by the close of 1877, it was increasingly clear to a reluctant Disraeli Government that the Zulus posed a major threat and could destabilise the whole region. Within twelve months, King Cetshwayo had been issued with an ultimatum demanding he disband the Zulu army and accept British rule. On 11 January 1879, British No. 3 Column invaded the native Zululand with a mix of regulars and white volunteers. It took six months to defeat the Zulus, but in so doing, British total control was consolidated over both Natal and the Transvaal.

On 16 December 1880, The Transvaal declared its independence from London; with the Zulu threat removed, the Boers could now raise defence solely against British governance. For a period of ten weeks, army garrisons were besieged and convoys attacked by Boer militia. The militia comprised mainly farmers whose expert handling of the horse and rifle made them very effective, mobile troops, in stark contrast to the very regimented approach adopted by the British. On 14 February, Kruger offered a solution to the conflict, but whilst London considered the offer, senior British officers on the ground decided to launch a further, decisive attack. On 26 February 1881, 360 British troops took up position on Majuba Hill overlooking a number of Boer positions. The following day, they were practically wiped out by accurate sniper fire, the Boers lost one man. A peace treaty was finally signed on 23 March 1881; the Boers would now hold self-governance, but the Queen would retain nominal reign.

Above left: Paul Kruger, President of the Transvaal from 1880.

Above right: Joseph Chamberlain in a painting by John Singer Sargent.

The uneasy peace was all but destroyed in 1886 when a rich deposit of gold was discovered at Witwatersrand around 30 miles south of the Boer capital Pretoria. This sparked a 'Klondike'-like gold rush, mostly from Britain. The Uitlanders (simply foreigner) soon outnumbered the Boer in the Transvaal. Tensions rose, leading to the failed Jameson Raid in 1895; Uitlanders, encouraged by the British and led by Leander Jameson, marched on Johannesburg. The march did not lead to insurrection as the colonialists had hoped. Meanwhile, the British Government had renewed its interest in a federation comprising both the Transvaal and Orange Free State, citing Uitlanders' rights but ultimately to control the new gold deposits. Negotiations failed and in September 1899 Joseph Chamberlain, British Colonial Secretary issued an ultimatum demanding equality for all incomers.

Sir Ellis Ashmead-Bartlett (Conservative)
I beg to ask the Secretary of State for the Colonies whether Her Majesty's Government have received confirmation of the grievous and unprovoked maltreatment and wholesale robbery of unarmed Uitlander civilians by armed Boers; and, if so, whether Her Majesty's Government will issue a proclamation stating their intention to hold the perpetrators of these outrages responsible for their brutality.

Mr J. Chamberlain (Liberal)

On the 11th instant I instructed the High Commissioner to warn President Kruger that he and his Government are expected to protect the lives and property of all peaceable persons, British subjects and others, and will be held responsible by Her Majesty's Government for any acts committed contrary to the usages of civilised people.

HC Deb 19 October 1899 vol. 77 cc237-8 237

Fearing the loss of any independence the Boers had already gained, President Kruger denounced the plan, giving British troops forty-eight hours to withdraw from the border of the Boer states. None was forthcoming and war was declared.

The two decades leading up to the Second Boer War were also a time when the great powers of Europe were increasingly developing a protective economic policy. The worsening situation in the Southern African States had been a regular topic for discussion in Berlin, primarily with regard to German interests. Kaiser Wilhelm II later stated in his memoirs, published in 1922, that the Transvaal was 'a little nation which was Dutch – and hence Lower Saxon-German in origin – and to which we were sympathetic because of the racial relationship'. Further, German connections in the southern states were well developed by the end of the century. A large number of German businessmen had travelled to the Transvaal when gold was first discovered, and a major rail link, financed by German investors, had quickly been built between Pretoria and the sea. The ports servicing the rail head were the termini for a number of large German steamship operators. And, on occasion, German battleships were stationed in Delagoa Bay to try and maintain more than a civilian presence in the area. So, naturally, whenever the British exerted pressure on the fledgling states, the Boers looked to Germany for support; increasingly, they received it. With another war looming, Germany saw an opportunity to expand her trading empire at the expense of London. Naturally, any empire required a strong navy to police and protect it, so it was not long before the subject was dominating the corridors of the Reichstag.

Key to any future naval expansion was Alfred Tirpitz (later von Tirpitz), the State Secretary of the Imperial Navy Office to Kaiser Wilhelm II. Tirpitz is acknowledged as the father of the (then) modern German Navy. Joining the service at sixteen, Tirpitz steadily rose through the ranks, often being seen as a risk taker. In the 1870s, he oversaw the development of torpedo technology and the application of it tactically. By 1888, he had attained the rank of captain and was transferred to Berlin to work on a new strategy for creating a High Seas Fleet; Tirpitz was a great advocate of the battleship, a stance that found favour with the Kaiser but initially had little impact on the Reichstag.

In 1897, Tirpitz lobbied the country to push through a Navy Bill designed to lift the German fleet to at least third ranking in world stakes. In June 1898, the German Navy League was formed with the aim of promoting sea power and to publicise the need for a large navy to protect both German industry and foreign trade routes. Crucially, Fritz Krupp and a number of other major manufacturers sponsored the endeavour. When the Bill reached the Reichstag for final reading on 23 March 1898, the statements centred on expanding German sea power through the construction of 'more and more battleships'. The Bill passed into law on 26 March.

Boer troops at Ladysmith in 1899.

With the outbreak of the Second Boer War in October 1899 all Germany could do was watch from the sidelines. No matter how outraged she was, the Imperial Navy was nowhere near large or powerful enough to make a challenge on the Boers' behalf. That said, many German factories were directed to supply the Boers with arms. Naturally, the British Government made assurances that German vessels would be free from molestation in African waters, mindful of the complications forcing the German hand would have. However, in January 1900, a number of German mail steamers were stopped off the African coast by the Royal Navy and searched for contraband. The Reichstag was incensed. The following Hansard extract explains:

Mr Gibson Bowles (Conservative)
I beg to ask the Under Secretary of State for Foreign Affairs is he aware that the boarding and prize officers of Her Majesty's ship *Thetis*, which detained the German ship *Herzog* on suspicion of carrying contraband of war, neither broke bulk nor made any search into or examination of the *Herzog*'s cargo; what was the nature of the summary search which is alleged to have taken place, by whom was it made, and in virtue of what authority; was it made before the *Herzog* was released by order of Her Majesty's Government, or after the release, and when and where was it made; and did those who conducted it examine the boxes marked 'Macaroni', which there is reason to believe contained rifles, and did they examine any other part of the cargo.

The Under Secretary Of State For Foreign Affairs Mr Brodrick (Conservative)
Bulk was not broken, nor could it properly be broken except under orders from a prize court. The reports received show that an examination of the papers on board relating to the cargo was made by the officers of Her Majesty's ship *Thetis* at sea on the 3rd of January. It was made before the ship was released. The boxes mentioned were not examined, but there is no reason to suppose that they contained rifles, as none were found at Lorenzo Marques, where a careful examination of the ship's cargo took place.

HC Deb 09 February 1900 vol. 78 cc1041-2

Tirpitz seized the opportunity and, on a wave of anti-British sentiment, drafted the Second Navy Bill. This time no publicity league was needed to raise the Bill's profile, and by 20 June 1900, it had passed through the Reichstag and become law. It is with the passing of this Bill that Germany embarks on the long road to war and consequently sets the clock running for the bombardment of the East Coast. Anti-German articles appeared in many newspapers around the same time, often fuelled by comments emanating from central Europe; however, not all had their origins in fact:

> Mr Nicol
> In the absence of the First Lord of the Admiralty I beg to ask the Financial Secretary a question of which I have given private notice, as to whether the attention of the Admiralty has been called to a statement in the public Press, that three cheers for the Boer Republics were given by the sailors of the German battleship *Deutschland*, at Portsmouth, under the eyes of their own officers, and whether there is any confirmation of this statement.
>
> The Secretary to the Admiralty, Mr Macartney (Irish Unionist)
> Yes, Sir, the attention of the First Lord of the Admiralty has been called to the statement contained in my hon. friend's question. He has caused inquiries to be made at Portsmouth, and as the result of those inquiries, he believes the report to be a pure fabrication without any foundation whatever.
> HC Deb 22 March 1900 vol. 81 cc34-5

The Second Navy Law proposed doubling the German fleet from nineteen battleships to thirty-eight, divided into four battle squadrons, two flagships and a number of reserve vessels. Interestingly, construction was to be completed by 1917. Importantly, the primary focus of this fire-power was to be the fleet of the Royal Navy.

> To protect Germany's sea trade and colonies in the existing circumstances, there is only one means: Germany must have a battle fleet so strong that even for the adversary with the greatest sea power, a war against it would involve such dangers as to imperil his own position in the world.
> Preamble to Second Navy Law
Translation from R. Massie, 1991, 181

Contained within the Second Law was a new concept to warfare – risk. Tirpitz wagered that the greater part of the British fleet would always be dispersed around the world protecting her interests, leaving the country strategically weak. A major engagement with the German battle fleet in the North Sea or North Atlantic would weaken the Royal Navy considerably, even if they were victorious. The hope was that either Russia or France would take advantage of this to disrupt Empire trade routes or take strategic ports from the British. There was always the possibility that the superior Royal Navy, if it realised what the Germans' plans were, would destroy the fledgling fleet whilst still under construction, a danger period estimated to last five years. Two years after the event, compensation was paid to the German Government for the detaining of the mail vessels, but by then the damage had been done and events had become unstoppable.

Mr Gibson Bowles (Conservative)
I beg to ask the Under Secretary of State for Foreign Affairs, can he state what is the total amount of compensation paid, or undertaken to be paid, up to date either to the German Government or to German subjects in respect of the detention and visit or search of German vessels suspected of carrying contraband of war to the King's enemies in South Africa; can he further give the number and names of the German vessels in respect of which any such compensation has been paid or promised. Can he state generally the grounds on which such compensation was claimed and allowed; and can he say out of what funds it has been provided.

The Under Secretary of State for Foreign Affairs, Lord Cranborne (Conservative)
A sum of £28,380 was paid in September, 1900, to the German Government, in respect of compensation for the seizure and detention of the three German mail steamers, *General*, *Bundesrath*, and *Herzog*; of the German sailing ship *Hans Wagner* and of the German barque *Marie*. This amount was arrived at after careful consideration by a joint Anglo-German Committee, which sat at the Foreign Office, and it was based on what appeared a fair and reasonable calculation of the expenses necessarily incurred. The amount so awarded was paid out of Navy Funds.

HC Deb 20 January 1902 vol. 101 c303

The Second Boer War was Britain's costliest adventure to date. Initially, the Boers made spectacular gains besieging a number of garrisons across the region and defeating British attempts to lift sieges at three other administrative centres. By 1900, the British had fielded a vast army drawn from all corners of the Empire; it brushed aside all resistance and took the major cities by the end of the year. With the campaign clearly

Alfred von Tirpitz (centre), father of the Imperial Navy. The Kaiser is on his left.

Right: Lord
Salisbury.

Far right:
Concentration
camps where
an estimated
25,000 Boer
women and
children died.

at an end, Lord Salisbury called what was to be known as the 'Khaki Election'; his
Unionist party romped home. The Boers, though, were not finished and conducted a
guerrilla campaign against the British forces for a further two years. Attacks on resupply
columns and garrisons, disruption of communications, individual assassinations and
general civil unrest were all employed. The British, used to fighting colonial wars often
against natives armed with little more than spears, were thrown into turmoil, adversely
reacting against the population at large. Now under the leadership of Lord Kitchener,
many farms were burnt, large areas of land (Veldt) were cleared of cattle and crops, and
Boer families were herded into specific areas known as concentration camps. Death
rates were high, especially amongst women and children, sparking off mass protests in
Britain. In fact, during a debate in 1904 on the employ of Chinese labour throughout
the Empire, Dr Thomas Macnamara, MP, for Camberwell North, quoted the figures
then known.

> The South African War lasted thirty-three months, it cost £250,000,000 of money,
> 25,000 British soldiers died, 25,000 came home permanently maimed, and quite
> another 25,000 women, children, and men must have died in the concentration
> camps, all for this, according to the Government.
>
> HC Deb 16 February 1904 vol. 129 cc1501-66

The Far East

Southern Africa was not the only part of the world causing concern in London. China,
with so many Western Nations still competing for influence through prohibitive leases
and trade concession, also threatened to descend into chaos. Western powers had, for
the last four decades, divided China up with railways and trade routes, Europeanised
vast swathes of the population, and taken control of many sea ports, to the detriment of
the Chinese Government. In June 1900, the situation boiled over into direct action by
China's peasant population in the north of the country. Their remit was simple: rid the
country of the foreigner, his industries, customs and, above all, clear away Christianity.

Boxers at Tientsin.

The peasant army called themselves 'Fists of the Righteous Harmony'; Britain knew them as the Boxers. A catalyst for the rebellion was the Germanisation of the city of Tsingtao, on lease to the Kaiser for ninety-nine years. Local Chinese opposition was met with burnt villages, and by 1899, the first pockets of armed resistance had appeared.

By mid-1900, thousands of Boxers were descending on the centre of Peking, or more accurately an area just off Tiananmen Square known as the Legation Quarter. It was here that the majority of foreign powers had their diplomatic offices. Concerned that something dangerous was brewing, especially since the Boxers were now burning villages and hacking to death any foreigner or Chinese Christian they came across, many mission heads asked their respective governments for military assistance. Around 400 marines made it to the city before, on 20 June, the Boxers surrounded the area with help from the Imperial Chinese Army; the siege was to last fifty-five days. By mid-July, the situation was desperate.

Sir H. Campbell-Bannerman (Liberal)
Can the right hon. Gentleman say whether he is obliged to confirm the terrible news we have received from China?

Mr Brodrick (Conservative)
No, Sir; we have no confirmation of the news. The telegraph is not working between Shanghai and Cheefoo. We are unable, therefore, to obtain any information at present. The land telegraph lines have been cut, and we are unable to hold any communication with our own naval officers at present.

HC Deb 13 July 1900 vol. 85 c1452

First attempts to lift the siege were not successful. Forts at the mouth of the Hai River at Ta-Ka and the city of Tientsin 15 miles inland were the first objectives required in the relief of the missions:

Mr Brodrick
The forts opened fire on the allied forces, but the operations of the Chinese in reinforcing Ta-ka, attacking Tong-ku, opposite Ta-ka and mining the mouth of the

Peiho [Hai] would have made it necessary in any case to seize the forts before the relief of Tientsin could be attempted.

HC Deb 13 July 1900 vol. 85 c1452-3

When the relief operation got underway, Vice-Admiral Sir Edward Seymour led a coalition force around 2,000 strong into the field. After the capture of Ta-ka, the force was transported by rail to Tientsin with the knowledge of the Chinese Government. Unfortunately, just over halfway between Tientsin and Peking, the trains were stopped by track removal; seen as vulnerable, the transport was then attacked by waves of lightly armed Boxers. Seymour was forced to retreat under fire, eventually digging in at the Great Hsi-Ku Arsenal, a facility some 9 miles from Tientsin. The arsenal was a major stockpile of German manufactured rifles and ammunition as well as medical and food supplies. After successfully getting word out, Seymour was eventually relieved on 25 June by a mixture of British and Russian troops.

Fortifications at Ta-ka were the first objective if any relief of the Legation Quarter was to be successful.

Marines from HMS *Alacrity*. Interestingly, this ship was commanded by Christopher Cradock, who was lost at the Battle of Coronel in 1914.

From mid-July 1900, a multi-national force began to assemble at Tientsin for another attempt to lift the siege in Peking. By then, western governments did not know whether anyone would still be alive. The British press had speculated as to the horrors that were being endured in the city, as all communications had been severed. On 14 August, British and Japanese troops entered Peking, lifting the siege, the Boxers and the Imperial army collapsed, and the city was all but abandoned. Whilst outwardly the operation was hailed a great success, internally European politics raged in the background. Germany, and moreover the Kaiser, was not pleased that Vice-Admiral Seymour had headed the first rescue attempt, and the second, successful, venture had been under a Russian Commander-in-Chief, General Linevitch, leaving Germany out of the limelight but still suffering casualties.

The Kaiser dispatched Field Marshal Count Waldersee and around 25,000 troops on 18 August to take command of the armies that now sat in Peking. By the time he reached the city, the campaign had ended; however, German troops set about exacting revenge for the death of their minister, who had been assassinated in the rebellion. Again, villages burnt and Chinese families were shot, only this time it was at the hands of the German Army. All the while, the Kaiser's intent was to extract the biggest reparations and indemnity possible from the Chinese Government, primarily to pay for the Second Navy Law that had recently passed through the Reichstag. It was not until June 1901 that German occupying forces began withdrawing from the city.

Peking, June 2. At a meeting of the Generals of the Allied troops to-day it was decided to transfer the administration of the City of Peking to the Chinese officials gradually during June.

Count von Waldersee, accompanied by his staff, will leave Peking to-morrow. Two special trains will run all week taking troops to Taku. The Germans are removing an extraordinary quantity of baggage, including Chinese carts, tables and chairs.

The New York Times, 3 June 1901

Russian Interest

Russia had substantially more to lose had the Boxers been successful. Bordering the country, they had been steadily acquiring an Eastern Empire through contracts and agreements with the Chinese Government. In late 1897, a Russian naval squadron sailed to Port Arthur, landed a detachment of marines, and raised the Imperial Flag. Then, from a strong position, they bullied the Chinese into granting the Russian Government a twenty-five-year lease on the port and railway construction rights across Manchuria. In so doing, they set themselves on the road to disaster.

The history of Port Arthur was complicated. The key to the northern Yellow Sea, it had been a major area of contention between China and Japan for years. After the Chinese army were defeated at Pyongyang in Korea, the Japanese army had crossed the Korean Bay to the Liaodong Peninsula, taking it and Port Arthur in November 1894.

The Central News Agency reported on the 24th, 'PORT ARTHUR HAS FALLEN; Japan Has the Key to the Capital of the Chinese Empire. NOW IT WILL BE PEKING OR PEACE Military Cities [Authorities] Considered the Fort as Far Superior to Gibraltar in Natural Resources of Defence.'

The seizure of Port Arthur and the increased Japanese influence over the Yellow Sea concerned many European powers. So much so that Russia, France and Germany, through a diplomatic initiative known as the 'Triple Intervention', exerted pressure on Japan to relinquish the port in lieu of an enhanced financial indemnity. The Japanese Government protested to other western powers but neither the United States nor Great Britain came to their diplomatic aid. So, on the 5 May 1895, Japan announced it was to hand back the peninsula and the port. The last troops left in December. The 'Triple Intervention' had an underlying remit. Russia was desperate to expand its influence and gains in Asia and a port in the Yellow Sea would allow easy access to the Pacific. The Japanese retention of Port Arthur would have scuppered the plan. France had no real interest in Northern China; however, it was concerned about the growing strength of Germany and could ill afford to be sidelined in major territorial discussions. Germany had aspirations of building an empire; however, it was 200 years behind the other European countries and subsequently needed the blessing or friendship of existing major powers. If Germany was to establish a major presence in China, it would need the support of the Russians, and this would only be forthcoming with reciprocal arrangements such as the 'Triple Intervention'.

The following two years were a disaster for the Chinese; western governments took the opportunity to force trade, territorial and political agreements on the ailing empire. All this was carried out under the nose of Japan, who had been forced to relinquish its military gains. And when the Russians had the audacity to 'steal' Port Arthur, then force a twenty-five-year lease on it, Japan started to re-arm. Port Arthur was the culmination of forty years of Russian expansion into China, especially Manchuria, and by the turn of the century, this was raising more than a few eyebrows in London. Sir Ashmead-Bartlett raised the issue in the House of Commons:

> There can be little doubt that the Russian Government is now pressing upon China a Convention which, if signed, would give our great rival in the Far East very important advantages over this country in regard to political power and commerce in the north-eastern portion of China.
>
> HC Deb 28 March 1901 vol. 92 cc163-96

Clearly, Russia had taken the opportunity during the Boxer Rebellion to increase its troop strength in Manchuria. And whilst other nations began withdrawing their forces, Russia continued to increase its presence. Ashmead-Bartlett explained:

> When Russia once obtains political and military control in Manchuria, and when the Trans-Siberian railway is completed, by which Russia can throw immense stores of munitions and hundreds of thousands of troops into Manchuria, we shall find ourselves in presence of that 'force majeure' which it will be impossible to deal with.
>
> HC Deb 28 March 1901 vol. 92 cc163-96

A major threat to Britain's extensive trade interests, estimated in 1900 to be 64 per cent of China's output, could ultimately destabilise the Far East's economy and have repercussions in India. What was needed was an ally in the east who could be relied on, only then might it be possible to counter Russian expansionism. Containment came on 30 January 1902 in London when an alliance between Britain and Japan was signed. The possibility of agreement had been present since Russia, leading Germany and France by the nose, had interfered in the peace talks at the end of the Sino-Japanese war. The Anglo-Japanese Alliance was a gamble for Britain, but clearly one worth taking. Until this agreement, London had pursued a foreign policy known to the world as 'Splendid Isolation'. At its core was the maintenance of the balance of power in Europe without entering into any binding agreements, especially those involving military assistance. When Germany unified in 1871 and proceeded to court potential allies on the Continent, it became increasingly apparent that the British could no longer follow the isolationist path. Russia was already following an aggressive expansionist policy in the east, Germany was building a navy that outwardly had the Royal Navy in its sights, and France, who had been in an alliance with Russia since 1892, were unlikely to side with the United Kingdom if conflict broke out.

The interference of Germany, Russia and France in the peace accord in 1895, clearly to fulfil Russia's aspirations in the region, had deeply humiliated the Japanese Government. But humiliation soon turned to anger and a determination to gain the upper hand militarily. The international effort against the Boxers had allowed the Japanese to work with Western powers; now an understanding with one would be extremely advantageous, especially if it were the British. The Anglo-Japanese Alliance was the perfect vehicle for both signatories according to the House of Commons debate on the subject.

Lord Cranborne (Conservative)
Of course it is only in defence of their respective interests as above described – that is, when attacked by the aggressive action of a third Power – that any obligation is thrown upon the ally. I need not say that whether the action is aggressive or not is a question for what I call the second Power, or ally, to determine. Either Power, before it undertakes any obligation, has a right to judge whether or not the conditions of the Treaty have been fulfilled. When such a case does arise the House will observe that the conditions are still very moderate. In the case of an attack by a single Power, all the ally is bound to do is to maintain neutrality; and to do its best to restrict the quarrel to the two Powers involved. It is only when another Power intervenes, when there is a coalition against either Great Britain or Japan, that the extreme obligation on the Ally of interfering by armed force comes into operation.
HC Deb 13 February 1902 vol. 102 cc1272-313

For the British, this was the end of Splendid Isolation in the East. It also meant that if Japan decided to take revenge on the Russians, Britain would be able to restrain the other powers through 'peace' negotiations whilst the Japanese went about their work. With luck, this would remove one of the major naval threats to Britain and in so doing substantially damage von Tirpitz' risk theory. The Royal Navy had, since 1870, been a major influence on the Imperial Japanese fleet; indeed, the British model had been followed by royal decree, giving Britain a worthy ally in the East if such a situation ever arose. British shipyards benefitted from Japanese contracts to the tune of six battleships, four armoured cruisers and two cruisers, sixteen destroyers and a number of torpedo boats. It would only be a matter of time before the Japanese were tempted to use their newfound might.

Russo-Japanese War

By mid-1903, Japan was actively pursuing the removal of Russian troops from Manchuria, increasingly creating alarm in the House of Commons. 'Have the Government any information to the effect that Japan is mobilising her forces and that an outbreak of hostilities in the Far East between that country and Russia is impending?' asked a house member in July 1903. Indeed, London was making 'frequent representations' to the Russian Government 'with regard to the delay in the evacuation of Manchuria'. By the turn of the year, there had still been no removal of Russian troops or equipment:

> Mr Aretas Akers Douglas (Secretary of State) (Conservative)
> We have been officially informed that diplomatic relations between the Governments of Russia and Japan have been broken off. As to the details I can add nothing to the information which appears in this connection in the public Press this morning.
>   HC Deb 08 February 1904 vol. 129 cc598-9

That same day the Imperial Japanese Navy attacked the Russian Far East Fleet lying at anchor in Port Arthur. A number of torpedo attacks disabled two Russian battleships; however, the Japanese found it difficult to get in close enough to do much further damage, as Port Arthur had been heavily fortified, protected by a number of large coastal batteries. By May 1904, Japanese ground troops, trained by the Germans, had landed at several points on the Manchurian coast, driving the Russians south into the Liaodong Peninsula. Keeping the pressure up at Port Arthur, the Japanese sunk a number of concrete-filled steamers around the deep-water channels to restrict access, sowed mines across the bay and continued torpedo attacks. Successes on land ensured by the end of June that Japanese artillery was within range of the port, and it proceeded to bombard the ships now trapped within. With such obvious attrition, the Russians decided to reinforce the Far East Fleet with ships from the Baltic Fleet; the problem was the Baltic Fleet was at anchor in its northern port – 18,000 miles away.

On 16 October 1904, the fleet left Libau, in what is now Latvia, under the command of Admiral Zinovy Petrovich Rozhdestvensky. Graduating from the Russian Sea Cadet Corps in 1868, he spent five years at artillery school and served with the Baltic Fleet as a gunnery officer. He saw action in the Russo-Turkish conflict of 1877 and served as Naval Attaché to Britain from 1891 to 1893. By 1902, he had been appointed Chief of Naval Staff with a specific interest in Russian involvement in the Far East.

Above left: Japanese siege guns were very effective against the ships in Port Arthur.

Above right: The Russian ships *Pallada* and *Pobeda*. Both were sunk by Japanese siege guns.

Damage to *Pobeda*. Note the coal sacks littering the deck.

The expedition got off to a poor start with two ships ramming each other and a further one running aground on the first day. Over the next few days, reports that the Japanese had stationed torpedo boats in the North Sea were disseminated around the ships. The crews, mostly undertrained, illiterate peasants often press-ganged into service, became increasingly jumpy, especially on hearing reports that they were under attack from torpedoes. Indeed, the men were later described – 'the only common factor among them was the crews' lack of naval knowledge and proficiency'. Matters were made worse by the fact that whilst in the North Sea the Baltic Fleet was close to Japan's ally, albeit that she was 'overtly neutral'. At any moment, the Royal Navy could appear and finish the fleet in its tracks.

The Dogger Bank Incident

War in the Far East had consequences for the East Coast of Britain too. On the night of 21 October 1904, a large flotilla of trawlers from the Gamecock Fleet, registered in Hull, was fishing on the Dogger Bank in the North Sea when the Russian Baltic Fleet attacked them. The attack caused an international incident, one that could have easily brought about a European war. As a precautionary measure, the Baltic Fleet had been divided into six separate squadrons, all heading for a re-coaling stop in Spain. On 21 October, the squadron comprising the First Battleship Division, mostly new battleships and cruisers, was making slow progress southward through a major fog bank. Bringing up the rear was the repair ship *Kamchatka*. At 20.55, she reported that she was under attack from at least eight torpedo craft; no torpedoes had been seen but the boats were coming from all sides; by 23.00 all had vanished. Shortly after that, the squadrons began to enter Dogger Bank, by now with guns manned ready for the enemy. The area was well known as a favourite British fishing ground; indeed, it was so popular, the Bank often proved difficult to navigate because of the dense number of ships.

This night was no exception; at least fifty ships of assorted shapes and sizes had nets in the water. Eyewitnesses later recalled the approaching Russian ships on two parallel courses, one of which would be right through the middle of the fishing fleet. Sensing disaster, the Hull fleet's 'Admiral' (senior fisherman) fired up green flares to indicate their collective position and to tell the trawlers to tack to starboard. On board the battleships, searchlights were turned on, illuminating what appeared to be Japanese torpedo boats bearing down on them, and the gunners opened fire. A measure of the chaos onboard the battleship *Orel* (*Oryol*) can be gleaned from the following account:

> The *Oryol* was humming like a hive of angry bees. Bugles blared, drums rumbled; rails rattled under the weight of hand trucks laden with shells; heavy guns were fired from the starboard and port turrets, lighting the darkness with flashes as they discharged and stirring the night with echoing thunder. Men swarmed on to shrouds and bridges. Discipline went west. Men yelled: 'Destroyers! The Destroyers!' 'Where are they?' 'A dozen at least.' 'No more than that' 'we're done for.'
>
> A. Novikoff-Priboy, written in 1937

The flares also attracted the attentions of the cruisers in the further squadron; naturally, they turned on the searchlights to investigate and were immediately fired upon by their own battleships. The captain of the cruiser *Aurora* quickly worked out that a fleet of torpedo boats could not lay down the amount of firepower he was currently experiencing. Clearly, he was being fired upon by his own comrades and with that he ordered the lighting of identification lamps, saving further damage. The trawlers had no such chance to protest their innocence.

One trawler, the *Crane*, was sunk, and two men died on the day, a further succumbing to his injuries some months later. The first recorded eyewitness account of the attack was given by a surviving crewmember of the *Crane* once on board the Mission Steamer

The Hull Trawler Outrage. The attack on the fleet by the Russian Navy on 21 October 1904 left three dead.

Joseph and Sarah Miles. Mission ships were often no more than fishing smacks owned by, or donated to, the Royal National Mission to Deep Sea Fishermen, but they had medical facilities, something often needed at the turn of the century, and especially so now.

> 'We had just hauled and shot away again,' he said, 'and were in the fish-pound cleaning the fish and passing jokes about the war vessels, which we could see quite plain, and heard their firing, when suddenly something hit us. The third hand said, "Skipper, our fish-boxes are on fire; I'm going below out of this," and walked forward, the skipper, who was on the bridge, laughing at him for being frightened. We were hit again forward, and some one called out and said, "The bosun is shot." I went forward to look, and found the boatswain bleeding and a hole through our bulwarks, and the fore companionway knocked away. I went to tell the skipper. Before I got aft a shot went through the engine-casing, and I began to feel frightened. I could see that the skipper was not on the bridge. I went aft, passed the chief, who was bleeding, gave him my neck-cloth to stop the blood, went right aft and saw the skipper lying on the grating. I said, "Oh, my God, he is shot!" I picked him up and saw that his head was battered to pieces. I dropped him, rushed down the forecastle, and saw the boatswain lying on the floor, with his head battered in.'

If the 'Dogger Bank Incident' demonstrated anything it was that the level of competence of the Russian Navy had been seriously overestimated. Notwithstanding the complete lack of geographical awareness the commanders had already displayed, by the time the fleet reached Dogger Bank, most crews were in a state of hysteria. When the order was given to open fire, thousands of rounds were expended on the trawler fleet, so much so that many ships had to restock with ammunition when it next put into port. For all the ordnance used, damage to the trawlers was surprisingly light, only really succeeding in injuring Russia's already dwindling reputation. The deed was reported internationally with many echoing the sentiment 'it will cast ridicule on the Russian Navy, which will not be confined to those immediately responsible.' By 24 October, the Russian Government was trying to limit the damage to their cause. The following piece reported in *The New York Times* demonstrates the level of desperation.

Russian Fleet Feared a Submarine Attack

It was stated today by a member of the Russian Embassy that the Russian Government had accurate information for months that Japanese Officers and seamen were in the United States and Great Britain busy on some problem of sea attack.

These Japanese officers have, according to what is declared to be accurate information, bought explosives and submarines in this country. One of these submarines has been transported by rail across the Continent to the Pacific Coast. Another is believed to be the submarine that was tried on the New England coast and mysteriously lost site of. It is said that this boat was taken to pieces and shipped across to England on a transatlantic steamer and assembled in a hidden harbour in one of the islands of the North Sea.

The New York Times, 25 October 1904

The British press and the House demanded action; the Royal Navy was readied for an interception of the Baltic Fleet at Gibraltar. Military action appeared likely. Russia and Britain already had a poor relationship, tarnished by the Crimean War and London's insistence on propping up Asiatic Turkey. War now appeared a real likelihood as far as the British press were concerned. On board the Russian vessels, the crews were blissfully unaware of the political storm brewing. Rozhdestvensky kept radio silence for four days in case they gave away their position. It was only when the fleet put into the friendly port of Vigo, Spain, that Admiral Rozhdestvensky told the government in St Petersburg of the encounter. He maintained that the action was warranted – the 'incident was occasioned by the action of two torpedo boats'. He went further, blaming the British trawlers: 'Our ships refrained from giving assistance to the trawlers on account of their apparent complicity, which they manifested by their persistence in attempting to pass through our line.' *Punch* had a warning for those still on the route of the Baltic Fleet:

As 'Ships of the Desert' are liable to be mistaken for Japanese torpedo-boats, the Egyptian government has warned all camel drivers that, during the passage of the Baltic Fleet through the Suez Canal, camels will be allowed within shell-range of the Canal only at their owner's risk. To remain near the Banks would be Suez-sidal.

Punch, 23 November 1904, p. 361.

France looked on nervously. She was Russia's only European ally at the time, and a war with Britain over the Dogger Bank would be disastrous. On 7 April 1904, the French had signed an agreement with her old enemy, effectively removing many of the colonial differences that both country's had endured. Crucially, the German Government had made no objections, welcoming the Anglo-French *Entente Cordiale*, although one clause covering Morocco would come back to haunt them later. Under the guidance of the Head of Foreign Affairs in Paris, Théophile Delassé, and the French Ambassador to London, Paul Cambon, an agreement had been reached that opened the door for both greater co-operation and further removed the need for 'Splendid Isolation'. The

Anglo-French *Entente Cordiale* also effectively removed France from the Two-Power Standard the Royal Navy maintained. Now this was under threat as France also had an agreement with the Russians – the Dual Alliance. Crucially, if Britain now attacked Russia over the incident, France would be obliged to joint forces with St Petersburg; if Russia forced the war, Paris would be forced to give material assistance. The situation was bleak no matter how it was viewed.

The answer came in the form of a Commission of Inquiry. Ambassador Cambon, after several days of diplomacy, ensured both sides would participate and, together with an international panel of naval experts sitting in Paris, the inquiry issued its findings on 25 February 1905.

> The majority of the commissioners express the opinion, on this subject, that the responsibility for this action and the results of the fire to which the fishing fleet was exposed are to be attributed to Admiral Zinovy Petrovich Rozhdestvensky.
>
> Section 11, para 6: Report of the commissioners appointed in conformity with Article 6 of the St Petersburg Declaration, November 12/25, 1904. Issued in Paris February 12/25, 1905.

Chiefly through the efforts of French diplomacy and the willingness of London to enter into the spirit of the Anglo-French *Entente*, war had been averted in Europe. It was not, however, to be the end of the Baltic Fleet or indeed Russia's troubles. Off the coast of West Africa, three more 'Japanese' ships were fired on, this time turning out to be Swedish, German and French vessels. Embarrassingly, these very ships were carrying coal to rendezvous points for the fleet; indeed, coal was to become a major problem for the Russians. Unfortunately for the fleet, the St Petersburg Government had recently described one of Britain's main exports as war cargo and likely to be confiscated as prize. London retorted if that were the case then Russian ships, especially from the navy, would not be welcome at any British-controlled port. Now, with an 18,000-mile journey ahead of them, where to refuel suddenly became a major issue. Even those countries friendly to Russia were bound by treaty not to help Russia whilst she was at war. The solution came through transferring coal at sea using German merchantmen; unfortunately, so much coal was loaded on the ships that the majority had to stay on deck. That which did not was stacked in cabins, bathrooms – in fact, anywhere that could take a sack. Soon everything was black, including the mood of the crews. Conditions on board began to take their toll; by the time the fleet docked at the appropriately named Hellville in Madagascar, mutiny was a real possibility. Suffering bad food, tropical heat, dysentery, cockroaches, rats, torrential rain coupled with three months of inactivity and lack of orders, discipline began to break down. Rozhdestvensky had been ordered to wait until the Third Baltic Fleet rendezvoused with his flotilla; however, he realised that if they lay at anchor for much longer, the whole fleet was exposed to mutiny. The prospect of a further squadron of Russian Navy ships navigating through the North Sea made everyone nervous; MPs in London and Hull were keen to gain assurances from the Russian Government.

Sir Seymour King (Conservative)
To ask the First Lord of the Treasury whether arrangements have been made to afford full protection to the fishing fleet on the Dogger Bank during the passage of the Russian third Baltic Fleet through the North Sea.

(Answered by Mr A. J. Balfour) (Conservative)
His Majesty's Government place implicit reliance on the assurance given by the Russian Government that they have taken every precaution to guard against the Recurrence of such incidents as that of 21st-22nd October, and that special instructions have been issued to the whole fleet with that object.

HC deb 22 February 1905 vol. 141 c890

Fearing the Baltic Fleet was on the point of collapse, Rozhdestvensky set sail for French Indochina, taking five weeks to get there. Again, he was ordered to wait for the Third Baltic Fleet, this time directly from the Tsar. Whilst the battle fleet crossed the Indian Ocean, one of the biggest land battles in modern history was taking place to the south of the Manchurian city of Mukden. The Tsar's army was practically eradicated on the field – 90,000 died. A decisive naval engagement was now the only way to counter the Japanese threat to Russia's eastern dreams.

In early May, both fleets met off the coast of China. They set sail for Vladivostok on 14 May; Rozhdestvensky hoped he would be able to affect some repairs there before engaging the enemy. It was not to be. As the fleet navigated the Korea Strait between the Japanese coast and Tsushima Island, they were spotted by a Japanese scout ship; soon four cruisers were shadowing. Intercepting radio transmissions indicating the main Japanese fleet, under the diminutive Admiral Tōgō Heihachirō, was on the way Rozhdestvensky readied his crews. Fleet Admiral Marquis Tōgō Heihachirō first saw action in 1863 during the Anglo-Satsuma war; the following year, the first Chinese Navy was formed and Tōgō joined. He went on to study naval sciences at Plymouth from 1871, giving him a valuable insight into the workings of the world's most modern navy. By 1903, he had been appointed Commander-in-Chief of the Imperial Japanese Navy.

In the Battle of Mukden, casualties were excessive. Here, Russian soldiers view Japanese dead; however, the Tsar's army had 90,000 killed.

The Russian Fleet met with disaster at Tsushima.

At 13.15, both fleets were visible, and after forty minutes of manoeuvring, Tōgō gave the order to engage; on the turn salvo after salvo was fired into the Russian fleet. By the morning of 15 May, the remnants of the Russian Navy, many having been picked off through the night by torpedo boats, were surrounded and forced to surrender. The losses were catastrophic; with the majority of ships sunk, severely damaged or captured, the Russian navy had been effectively removed from the world stage. The blow to Russian prestige was incalculable; not only had it been removed as a credible military power through the Far East adventure, the disaster further set the conditions for revolution.

In London, the predicament the Russians had found themselves in had been carefully monitored. The stakes were high; if Japan withdrew from the war with Russia then Britain would have an additional defensive problem in the Indian Ocean, as Japan would not be able to keep the Tsar in check. By early 1905, indications were that should the Japanese engage the Russian Navy they would do well, especially since damaging the Russian Fleet in the blockade of Port Arthur.

> It is well known that the two-power standard has always applied to France and Russia. One of these Powers, as we all know, has met with the greatest possible of disasters. It is difficult to ascertain the full extent of Russia's enormous losses in the war with Japan, but I think I am under the mark when I say that she has lost five battleships and five cruisers.
>
> HL Deb 21 March 1905 vol. 143 cc600-26

The Two-Power Standard had been a central part of the Naval Defence Act 1889, championed by Lord Salisbury, passed through Parliament 31 May that year. It was the largest expansion of the navy during the reign of Victoria, costing £21,500,000 over a five-year period. Ten battleships, thirty-eight cruisers, eighteen torpedo boats and a number of smaller vessels were placed on the order book. Prior to this, policy had demanded a navy one third larger than its nearest rival, now the Royal Navy was required to have twice the strength of the next two contenders – by the end of the

Admiral Tōgō Heihachirō.

nineteenth century, this was France and Russia. However, it was widely recognised that superiority in numbers did not guarantee victory.

> The Japanese navy, for the three years preceding the Russo-Japanese war, cost only £10,000,000, where as the Russian Navy, which was practically annihilated, cost £35,000,000 for the same period. It was not expenditure that secured efficiency.
>
> Finance Bill Debate
> HC Deb 05 June 1905 vol. 147 cc729-79

With the destruction of the Russian Fleet at Tsushima Island, a major thorn in Britain's side had been removed. More importantly, the Japanese Navy had been able to demonstrate that large-calibre gunnery could be extremely effective. Further, the Royal Navy had a number of 'observers' onboard Admiral Tōgō's fleet, and had witnessed first hand how the awesome power of large-calibre weapons could turn the tide of battle. On the day the Baltic Fleet had run into the Hull trawlers, incidentally Trafalgar Day, Admiral John 'Jackie' Fisher entered the Admiralty as First Sea Lord. Now the Royal Navy would have a driving force the like of which a generation had not seen. He favoured the large-calibre, high-speed combination for battleships, was committed to modernisation, and saw German as the next credible threat to Britain's naval supremacy. His appointment to the Admiralty set in motion the train of events that would accelerate the naval arms race and make the bombardment of the East Coast inevitable.

Three

'The Dreadnought,' says another expert, 'will make all other battleships obsolete.'

Jackie Fisher

John Arbuthnot (Jackie) Fisher was born in Sri Lanka (formally Ceylon) on 25 January 1841, the son of a British Army captain. After his father resigned his commission and became a less-than-successful coffee plantation owner, Fisher was moved to the home of his maternal grandfather in London. In 1854, at the age of thirteen, he entered the navy as a cadet serving on HMS *Victory*. By the end of July, Fisher had joined ship of the line HMS *Calcutta*; a sail ship with a complement of over 700, she saw service in the Crimean War, earning Fisher the Baltic Medal. He was later to see action, this time in the China Seas, during the Second Opium War (1856-60); Fisher very quickly became an expert in weaponry and spent a considerable amount of time at Portsmouth developing torpedoes and, more importantly, gunnery techniques.

During this period, he had one tour on HMS *Warrior*, the Royal Navy's iron battleship, before returning to shore duties as a gunnery instructor. He was promoted to captain in September 1876, taking command of a number of vessels before taking the bridge on HMS *Inflexible*, a brand-new ship that unfortunately for the progressive Fisher still carried sail and muzzle-loading guns. After further tours at HMS *Excellent*, the navy's gunnery school, and a number of commands, Fisher was promoted to Director of Naval Ordnance, becoming an Admiral in 1890.

With this promotion came Fisher's first meaningful contact with the production of fleet ships. It was not long before he had increased the construction effort, shaving a year of the build time off HMS *Royal Sovereign*; she was launched in two years. In 1892, Fisher was involved in the development of a class of anti-torpedo boat ships; the French had been building vast fleets of torpedo boats as a cheap alternative to battleships, coining the name destroyers.

On 31 August 1903, he took over as Commander-in-Chief of the naval base at Portsmouth, his flagship becoming HMS *Victory*. Beyond the duties encompassing training, construction, repair, and naval gunnery that came with the post, Fisher also took great interest in submarines. Fisher unleashed an interesting dichotomy; by developing the submarine into an effective weapon, he was also signposting the Royal

Right: John 'Jackie' Fisher as a midshipman.

Far right: Fisher just before he became First Sea Lord in 1904.

Navy's one major weakness. A lesser power could quite easily wreak havoc amongst a surface fleet with a squadron of such vessels. The attitude of the Admiralty changed from one of scornful rebuke to one of major concern over the next few years as the true potential of the submarine was demonstrated. This apparently emerging threat was to be top of Fisher's agenda as he entered the Admiralty on 21 October 1904 (Trafalgar Day) as First Sea Lord, and he had a plan on how to deal with it.

Dreadnought

Fisher recognised that distance and speed were the two key elements any commander should have available to him. These dictated when and where to fight, when to withdraw and influenced the time and method of engagement. The principles were simple. A fast ship could hold off engagement until the circumstances were in her favour (this was to be expertly demonstrated in 1914 at Coronel by von Spee). When blockading, speed was also a distinct advantage: any ship making a run from port was far more likely to be caught and the distances covered quicker allowed the ship to be out of range of submarines and coastal batteries for longer periods. If this was coupled with eight or ten large, same-calibre guns, the combination became lethal. Coastal bombardments could be carried out at ranges well beyond anything the defenders could muster. The same went for action at sea. A targeted vessel could be destroyed at ranges far beyond those she herself was capable of firing over. The dreadnought was, to all intents and purposes, designed to sail the seas with impunity.

On 22 December 1904, Fisher formed the Committee on Design, populated with forward-thinking, like-minded men, to put his concept at least on the drawing board. Sticking rigidly to the main points, guns and speed, the committee sat until the end of February 1905. Uniformity in gun power was the main priority. Currently, battleships were armed with an array of different-calibre guns, a situation that had as much to do with advances in technology as anything else. As new ships were commissioned, they had the latest guns fitted; however, the standard, more-proven systems were naturally incorporated as well. This steady march in technology had a detrimental effect of the ship's overall capability. A multitude of different-calibre shells needed to be stored on board, reducing the time the ship could remain at greater distances and thus reduced the obvious advantage of heavy fire power further from the target.

Mixed calibre had one further disadvantage; in the heat of battle, the commander was likely to use all available means to defeat the enemy, including all large calibres on board. One of the basics of gunnery was to observe where the shells were landing and adjust accordingly. The problem was different-sized shells require different elevations to achieve the same distance; unfortunately, the splashes around the target could often not be deciphered. A salvo from the same calibre removes that problem. During the rout of the Russian Navy at Tsushima in 1905, this assumption had been borne out. Royal Naval observers had reported that the accuracy given by large calibres coupled with the safe distances at which the Japanese Navy operated systematically destroyed the Russian battle fleet whilst experiencing next to no damage themselves.

Distance also removed the dreadnought beyond the effective range of fledgling submarines, although an armoured belt was to be fitted below the waterline in case a torpedo boat got in close. Interestingly, the effectiveness of submarines was little understood and, for that matter, not thought to be something worth worrying about:

Sir John Leng (Liberal)
– said a submarine was really a mechanical fish, with this difference, that they could not put into it the eyes of a fish to show where it was going. The periscope was a most ineffective instrument, and he doubted whether the Admiralty's steam fish would be really serviceable for naval purposes.

HC Deb 29 June 1905 vol. 148 cc552-98

HMS *Dreadnought* was also to be constructed differently. The internal areas of the hull were segregated with no chance of access between one section and another. Traditionally, crews had access to all parts of the ship via hatchways and doors, both between decks and from bow to stern. When the ship was in action, these doors were closed, sealing each area; however, their incorporation dictated this was still a weakness. When HMS *Victoria*, one of the largest battleships afloat, was rammed by HMS *Camperdown* off Syria in 1893, she had the majority of her watertight doors open. She sank in less than fifteen minutes taking 358 crew with her; *Dreadnought* would have self-contained sections built from the outset – that way, if the hull were holed, it would not necessarily mean the loss of the entire vessel. Interestingly, mines were not really seen as a threat to the colossal ship; again, many considered them a passing folly, not worthy of the Royal Navy. This view would prevail until the outbreak of the First World War and contribute to the loss of the super-dreadnought HMS *Audacious* off the coast of Ireland to just one mine in 1914.

It was not just the design of the battleship that Fisher revolutionised, he also had a major impact on the way manufacturers approached defence contracts, and in so doing, further intensified the arms race. A number of shipyards around the country

This page: HMS *Dreadnought* under construction.

were capable of building HMS *Dreadnought*; however, building at the Portsmouth Naval Yard allowed Fisher to dictate manning levels and the hours they worked. Currently, the time spent building a major-sized ship at Portsmouth was around two and a half years; Fisher reduced that to just a single year. This was a turning point, one that was to resonate throughout the twentieth century; speed in production would be the key to winning any arms race. True, you had to be innovative from the outset, but building one groundbreaking weapons platform is only the start – producing substantial numbers of them lies at the centre of success. With faster production comes a better-organised system of manufacturing; rather than buying each component as and when required, they were bought in ahead of time and stockpiled ready for use – this alone shaved months off the construction calendar.

All this was very well, but it was the effects HMS *Dreadnought* had on the world, especially those powers with aspirations of their own, that really shook the establishment to its very foundations. At one strike of the draftsman's pencil, the advantage the Royal Navy had over any potential enemy was gone. Now the Italians, Japanese, French, American and, more worryingly, German fleets, if they had the manufacturing capability, would be starting to re-arm on an equal footing.

> Earl Spencer (Liberal)
> We have now what is called the Two-Power standard. It did very well for a certain time; but I venture to say that at the present our naval force exceeds immensely the Two-Power standard. I dislike bringing other Powers into this matter, but it is well known that the Two-Power standard has already applied to France and Russia. One of these Powers, as we all know, has met with the greatest possible disasters. Therefore, the Two-Power standard has broken down.
>
> HL Deb 21 March 1905 vol. 143 cc600-26

On 29 June 1905, the Navy Estimates for 1905/06 were debated in the House of Commons. The key theme involved the financing of older vessels on reserve and the maintenance of those to be kept in service on the front line. It rapidly became clear that, over the last decade, technology had advanced to such a degree as to render much of the fleet obsolete, even before *Dreadnought* left the drawing board.

With the destruction of the Russian fleet and subsequent collapse of the Two-Power Standard, a new friendship agreed with the French and reforms being pushed through by the First Sea Lord 'Jackie' Fisher, it was inevitable that ships would have to go. Naturally, this brought about quite a stir, not least in Westminster, but most realised that it was unavoidable. As Viscount Goschen eloquently described,

> Many of these ships have been fine ships in their day. The rubbish of one day has been the glory of another; and it is melancholy to reflect that vessels that have been the pride and darling of their period come to be laid on one side as useless in this way.
>
> HL Deb 21 March 1905 vol. 143 cc600-26

This page: 'Britain's Mysterious Battleship Launched', 'Giant Dreadnought May Revolutionize Naval Warfare', 'Biggest and Fastest Afloat', said contemporary newspapers.

HMS *Victoria* sinks after being rammed by HMS *Camperdown* in 1893.

Nevertheless, the fact was the Royal Navy had accumulated a vast reserve of ships that would cost more to generate during times of crisis than the careful planning of their phasing out. True, there was always going to be some obsolescence, especially in the face of rapid technological advancements, but this could be planned for. However, obsession with the navy's size, partially driven by the Two-Power Standard, ensured a sizable chunk of the budget was being spent on redundant ships. Indeed, by 1906, the repair of the entire fleet was costing the country £4.8 million per year, just to mark time on size.

> Sir Charles Dilke (Liberal)
> Vessels built for war, armed for war, and prepared for war, were sold off because they could not stand against armoured cruisers, whilst the Estimates still bore a charge of thousands of pounds for subsidies to certain companies in order that we might have a call on their ships, which could not stand up against the armoured cruiser.
> HC Deb 29 June 1905 vol. 148 cc552-98

As part of Fisher's modernisation, the building programme was radically reshaped. In 1905, only one battleship was to be built, *Dreadnought*; unfortunately, the Committee of Designs felt unable to inform Parliament exactly what they had proposed. Interestingly, the *Times Engineering* supplement had no such problem; the month before, it published some leading particulars including armament, displacement, speed and power plant along with information on a number of other destroyer-orientated projects. Therefore, *Dreadnought* was laid down on Monday 2 October 1905; by 9 February 1906, the hull had been completed and was ready for launch. The headlines said it all: 'Britain's Mysterious Battleship Launched', 'Giant Dreadnought May Revolutionize Naval Warfare', 'Biggest and Fastest Afloat, to be driven by turbines – Result of Lessons Learned in the Russo-Japanese War'. After fitting out throughout the summer, she was ready for sea trials – one year and a day after she had been laid down! The Royal Navy took her on strength on 2 December 1906.

Of the many problems facing the German Navy, the most difficult to reconcile was the speed at which international politics changed direction. From the end of the Second Boer War, international events drove a complete shift in the way the world was politically mapped. Not least the rise of the Japanese, removal of the Russian Navy and rapid improvement in Anglo-French relations. Indeed, the speed was so great that Tirpitz' risk theory seemed the only constant policy in Europe; by doggedly following it, the German nation was committed to a policy that would ultimately lead them to ruin.

The German Navy had begun considering the implications of a large, same-calibre platform for their own fleet when an assessment of HMS *Dreadnought* appeared in *Jane's* (an annual reference book dealing with all aspects of armament). With the revelation that the vessel could at least match the strength of any two existing capital ships, it was time to take notice. What was to slow the production of similar vessels in the Baltic shipyards was not so much the Reichstag's reluctance to finance the venture but the size of the Kiel Canal (Kaiser-Wilhelm-Kanal). By August 1906, Berlin was reporting its own building programme to the world: 'German Battleships to Beat Dreadnoughts, Weight and Rapidity of their Fire are to be Greater.' The race was on. The press was also reporting that the first German submarine had been launched that same month and surveying work around the principle shipbuilder's premises and Kiel Canal pointed to further expansion. The reader will remember the German Navy League formed in June 1898 and subsequent Navy Laws pushed through the Reichstag around the time of the Second Boer War, all with the intention of countering British naval dominance. To ensure this was achieved, Tirpitz had convinced both the Kaiser and Reichstag that three capital ships were required every year. Aiming for the converted 2:3 ratio, this would use Britain's Two-Power Standard against her. Aiming for a sixty-strong battleship fleet inside twenty years would stretch British manufacturing to the limit, as there was no way she could build ninety battleships. The Royal Navy also relied on volunteers for service coming forward whilst conscription in Germany would ensure all ships were fully manned. Increasing the German fleet size would also force the Royal Navy to reinforce its world footprint, spreading itself ever thinner, a situation exacerbated by a number of countries entering the shipbuilding race. With the introduction of HMS *Dreadnought*, much of this careful planning was swept aside – only if Germany also built such leviathans could the great plan still be enacted. One of the first major moves was improving access to the North Sea, and additional legislation was needed if it was to proceed:

Above left: The depth of the Kiel Canal limited the German construction programme.

Above right: The Germans eyed the *Entente Cordiale* with suspicion.

Kiel Canal to be Deepened. Berlin, April 27. – The supplementary appropriation bill introduced in the Reichstag to-day provides $3,750,000 to be expended in widening and deepening the Kiel Ship Canal. The new depth will be thirty-six feet, and the total cost of the improvements is estimated at $55,250,000.

The New York Times, 28 April 1907

The Kiel Canal was critical to naval operations and had been the first step on the way to Germany's bid to become a world power. Opened on 21 June 1895, the canal was an economic godsend for both military and trade traffic, as it saved a journey of 520 miles around the Danish coast, often in the grip of violent storms. The problem was that, at 73 feet wide by 30 feet deep, it was just not big enough to carry dreadnought-sized vessels. Eventually the depth was re-cut to 37 feet and the width 147 feet by an army of 5,000 labourers. Whilst this was underway, the shipyards continued work on current projects, as it was still unclear what the British were actually building in Portsmouth dock. Faced with a dilemma, Tirpitz decided the way forward – in true Teutonic style – was to continue building five Deutschland-class battleships, with the advent of the *Dreadnought*, now outclassed, rather than put the work on hold. By the time the five battleships had been commissioned in 1908, British dockyards were already constructing a further nine dreadnought-class ships for the Royal Navy.

When the Anglo-French *Entente Cordiale* agreement was reached in April 1904, it effectively removed the reason for the Two-Power Standard to be applied in Europe. Later that year, the Russian Fleet suffered such a massive blow that the other possible belligerent had also gone. By the time the Anglo-Russian agreement had been reached in 1907 (a looser version of the agreement with France), it was clear that Germany's overt challenge to the Royal Navy had turned her neighbours against her and subsequently ended 'Splendid Isolation' – the British were now inextricably involved in European affairs.

Worldwide Effects

Naturally, the effects of any arms race are far reaching. New technology always allows others to follow suit and the introduction of HMS *Dreadnought* was no exception. The established industrial nations such as France and the United States saw the development as an opportunity to modernise whilst for a number of smaller nations it might now be possible to punch above their weight if they could build such a ship or secure one through a third party. The development of the world's navies at the turn of the century was also a symptom of the continuing shifting of power through industrialisation, probably best demonstrated by Japan. It is interesting that this lower stratum of naval development also drove the British policy makers in Whitehall. As independent countries, they posed little threat, but through alliance, mutual agreement and treaty, this threat could become real. The Mediterranean, for example, was bordered by a number of countries with credible navies, among them France, Italy and Austria, followed closely by Greece and Turkey. Building programmes during the first decade of the twentieth century were subsequently monitored with more than just passing interest. Any expansion of naval power had the possibility of directly affecting British trade routes, if not immediately then in the future, and thus had implications for the distribution of the Royal Navy in the region.

The French Navy was by far the biggest in the Mediterranean after the Royal Navy. The 'old enemy' had been one of the targets of the Two-Power Standard; however, by 1905, her North Sea and Channel operations had been eclipsed by the relentless output of the German shipyards, and so it was to the Mediterranean that she looked for dominance. Her main rivals were the Austrians and Italians, both competent constructors, but also bitter rivals more likely to fight than uphold any agreements. In the event, Italy eventually sided with France and Britain in the First World War, probably conscious that conflict with Britain would close down most of Italy's access to the sea. However, in 1905, as one of the signatories of the Triple Alliance, it appeared Italy could be a rival of France. The Triple Alliance had been signed in 1882; each signatory would support the others if they were attacked by two other powers. However, each would go to the other's aid if attacked by France alone. The Austrians, for their part, began building dreadnought-type ships around this time, converting from a coastal to a blue-water capability in the process. The Italians followed suit, whilst the French looked on with alarm. It was well known in Paris that neither side really saw 'eye to eye'; however, if the two new fleets were to combine against France, she would probably come off worse. Successive governments having the lack of foresight required to push through expensive modernisation programmes did not help this position of weakness. That lack of political will meant it was not until 1910 that French dockyards started building dreadnought-level ships, by then, those considered rivals had the

The *Connecticut*, part of the United States 'Great White Fleet'.

types at sea. The Italians, for their part, were one of the instigators of the 'all through calibre' dreadnought, but it took until 1909 before the Italian Government funded the construction of the type. In true innovating style, the *Dante Alighieri* was an advanced development carrying triple-gunned turrets; unfortunately, the Italian steel-production capability forced ship completion to be far slower than her rivals. However, it was not the Italians who caused most concern.

Until the turn of the century, the navy of the Austro-Hungarian Empire had been little more than a coastal protection fleet; in 1907, this changed with the laying down of three *Radetzky*-class semi-dreadnoughts (similar speed and armour to British type but reduced main calibre), followed up in 1910 by dreadnoughts proper. Both British and French governments looked on with renewed concern. Austria, also a signatory of the Triple Alliance, was most likely to honour the agreement, siding in any major conflict with Germany. Now the picture became confused. Italy, considering this possible alliance with Germany, sought assurances that the Austrians would not view Italy as a potential rival in the Mediterranean. For good measure, the German Navy, which was extremely anxious to see an agreement reached, dispatched two ships, crucially each more powerful than anything the French currently operated, into the Mediterranean. An altogether unholy alliance now grew. The only way the French Navy would be able to keep anywhere near a modicum of superiority in the Mediterranean would be if the Royal Navy intervened. In the event, the Italian Navy remained out of the early war, allowing the British–French coalition to rule the surface fleets. Add to this the smaller Turkish and Greek construction efforts from 1911, and it is not too difficult to see how the Mediterranean became the focus of much naval debate for a great number of countries. Interestingly, the growing tension between Turkey and Greece throughout the last few years of peace drove the Russians to restart their building programme. Turkey commissioned a dreadnought, to be built in Britain, in 1913, and acquired another, also being built in Britain, when Brazil was unable to pay for her. This acquisition forced the Russians to start building for the defence of the Black Sea.

Further afield, other major powers were building. The United States, stating its isolationist intent, had been slow to build up a modern navy and was unlikely to be a major threat to world peace or the European Powers at least for another decade. That said, in December 1907, President Theodore Roosevelt dispatched sixteen ships to circumnavigate the world. Primarily as a demonstration of American naval prowess, they took thirteen months, in four legs, to achieve it. The ships had their hulls painted white, earning them the nickname 'Great White Fleet'. It was the ultimate PR coup. Ignoring the majority of European powers, the United States fleet made sure they visited other emerging nations, including those that bordered the Pacific. 'Brilliant End of World Cruise' boasted the front page of The New York Times on the morning of 23 February 1909. It was not until 1916 that American shipyards would final lay down a full dreadnought. The only other up-and-coming major player that should be mentioned is Japan. They had proven to the world that a newly industrialised country was capable of great things. Destroying the naval capability of the Russians and brokering an alliance with the British meant they had become the strongest force in the Pacific. They, like the United States, were slow to initiate a battleship modernisation programme, only getting underway once the First World War had broken out.

We Want Eight and We Won't Wait

The problem with a major re-armament programme is cost. The national finances have to be in robust shape if vast investment is to underpin the programme unhindered, practically all other government functions must take second place. Unfortunately, in the Edwardian period, Liberals had other ideas, and social reform was at the top of their agenda. Emerging from an extended period of dour Victorian values and lack of ability to tackle poverty on a wide front, the Liberals grasped the concept of national 'welfare' with both hands; the problem was how to pay for it. On the death of Gladstone in 1898, the Liberals gained a new leader, Sir Henry Campbell-Bannerman, and with it a renewed chance to form a majority government. However, the party had been divided, especially over the plight of the Boers, rifts that would take time to heal. When the Leader of the Unionists, Lord Salisbury, called a snap election, the 'Khaki Election' as it was known, taking advantage of successes in South Africa, it was done with the knowledge that the Liberals were in no state to mount a credible challenge. By late 1905, election again looked imminent, as the Unionists had steadily conceded a large number of seats through by-elections forced by resignations over import duties. Meanwhile, the Liberals had resolved a number of major arguments within the party in the preceding years and were in a far better position to mount a challenge; their only weakness was Campbell-Bannerman himself. Unfortunately, Campbell-Bannerman, whilst the consummate political leader, was not a strong politician – any debate would surely see the opposition triumph after giving him a savaging. With that in mind, leading names in the Liberals took the initiative, dividing the responsibilities of government should the outcome of the election go their way. Asquith would become Chancellor of the Exchequer; Haldane the Lord Chancellor and Grey would to the Foreign Office. The election in January 1906 was a landslide in the Liberals' favour, enjoying an 88 majority.

Above left: Sir Henry Campbell-Bannerman.

Above right: Herbert Asquith.

Above left: Richard Haldane (centre).

Above right: David Lloyd George.

On Campbell-Bannerman's death in 1908, Herbert Asquith assumed the position of Prime Minister, immediately driving forward legislation to deal with some of the major welfare issues. Free school meals, old age pensions and, in 1911, the long-awaited National Insurance Bill, the foundation stone of the modern welfare state, all increased the state's liability to its citizens. In the process, national expenditure increased. Indirect taxation was the only way to counter the deficit argued the Unionists; Asquith disagreed, and when his Chancellor, David Lloyd George, delivered the budget for 1909, there was outcry. Lloyd George proposed a 'super tax' on the incomes of the very rich and attempted to bring in a land tax, again aimed at the wealthy. Championed as 'the people's budget', Lloyd George hit a number of areas that would affect only the well off, with a few notable exceptions, tobacco and alcohol being primary; petrol and motor taxes were introduced, licences for public houses appeared and income tax was set at 4 per cent to 6 per cent dependent on earnings. The House of Lords, cajoled by Unionist representation, threw the budget out. However, this was a dangerous tactic, as within a year the fight-wary government had passed the Parliament Act of 1911, limiting the Lords' veto to two years. Now legislation would be passed, if a little slowly.

Social welfare aside, the cost of maintaining an advantage over the current German naval expansion was becoming ever more expensive. The financial commitment had to take in all aspects of the building programme; any innovation in design, construction or weaponry often required new plant or a major redesign of the dockyard. Since a shortage of skilled workers had manifested itself, the wages bill had increased and further increases in the pay of navy staff were required in an attempt to retain sailors in the service. All this went against the Liberal manifesto pledge to reduce military spending. To Lloyd George, the answer was simple: reduce the number of ships being laid down and a three-year commitment to spending £7 million was removed. One dreadnought was cut from the programme in 1906, a further in 1907, and two more in 1908. The new First Lord of the Admiralty, Reginald McKenna, could stand by no longer. Whilst the British Government were making ever-deeper cuts into the Naval Estimates, the German shipbuilders had been trying to keep pace with the substantial orders placed through the Navy Law legislation. The balance in favour of the Royal Navy was clearly in jeopardy. McKenna estimated that by 1912 the margin would by thirteen German to sixteen British, clearly not a big enough margin when any overseas commitments were considered. The problem was now how to get an increased spending programme through the House. Indeed, by 1907, MPs had become increasingly militant over the dreadnought-building programme: 136 petitioned the Prime Minister prior to that year's estimates; the following year, 144 MPs raised similar concerns. The problem for the navy was that these demands for a reduction in expenditure were on top of the swingeing cuts the Liberal administration had already imposed. On 8 December, the First Lord of the Admiralty had bad news for the Cabinet: the German construction programme was far more advanced than first thought. The press and those in opposition exaggerated the shortfalls. The Conservatives went on the offensive, demanding, 'We want eight and we won't wait!' In their opinion, all had to be laid down at once – it was the only way the German acceleration could be countered. Indeed, the by-election at Croydon was fought exclusively on the eight-dreadnought ticket.

Sir Edward Grey.

By the middle of March 1909, the debate turned to just what would be the effect of increasing the Royal Navy's dreadnought numbers. Edward Grey, Foreign Secretary, discussed the situation in the House on 29 March. Germany had, by now, a huge land army and militarily – this was far more important to the Reichstag than a world-class navy. Britain, however, needed a global naval presence in order to ensure the Empire, and more importantly, the trade routes around the world were kept free of interference. As long as both respected each other's territories and international interests, then peace should prevail. However, if Germany continued to build a new navy at the current rate, peace would be threatened. War would probably become a reality if either Britain or Germany followed an isolationist policy against the other. That said, for Britain not to keep ahead of Germany's construction programme was to lose the world position she had built over the last 300 years. Any further talk of reductionism needed to be silenced before damage was done to the national image; the dreadnought-building programme was to be increased under a Liberal administration after all. There was one glimmer of hope:

Sir Edward Grey (Liberal)

If I was asked to name one thing which would mostly reassure the world – or reassure Europe – with regard to the prospects of peace, I think it would be that the naval expenditure in Germany would be diminished, and ours would follow suit, and be diminished also. Were there a cessation of competition in naval expenditure public opinion everywhere would take it as a guarantee of the good intentions of the two nations, and the effect would be incalculable.

HC Deb 29 March 1909 vol. 3 cc39-149

'It is running shipbuilding like an express train – to the minute.'

The navy estimates debated in the House of Commons on 3 August 1909 were a lively affair. It is often the case that, when discussing reductions or increases in budgets, the full implications are seldom considered, especially when the subject is emotive, and in 1909, they didn't come more emotive than the discussion surround the by-now-astronomical cost of maintaining the world lead in battleships.

> Lt-Colonel Wilfrid Ashley (Conservative)
> By deferring the laying down of the ships the Government will undoubtedly defer until April, 1912, a much needed addition to our 'Dreadnought' fleet, which, if they gave the orders at once, might be added in November, 1911. What is, perhaps, equally important, they may also cause a great congestion of shipbuilding in 1910-11, and thereby delay the speedy completion of ships which are urgently required for the fleet.
>   What is the shipbuilding programme of the Government? They say that in April, 1911, we shall have 12 'Dreadnoughts'; in July, 1911, 14; in November, 1911, 16; and in April, 1912, 20. That is running it very fine indeed. It is running shipbuilding like an express train – to the minute.
>   HC Deb 03 August 1909 vol. 8 cc1711-804

It was not just a matter of reducing the number of dreadnoughts to be built, all the forward planning and advance ordering, so much a part of Fisher's original production plan, would need to be slowed and then the shipyards would suffer, crucially along with a large number of voters and government supporters. Beyond that, the amount of national expenditure was without precedence:

> W. P. Byles (Liberal)
> It is true to say that half the national wealth of half the nations of Europe is being spent on what is after all, preparations to kill each other. Surely the extent to which this expenditure has grown has become a satire and a reflection on civilisation. Not in our generation perhaps, but if it goes on at the rate at which it has recently increased, sooner or later I believe it will submerge that civilisation and lead to national bankruptcy.
>   HC Deb 03 August 1909 vol. 8 cc1711-804

This was not a solid Liberal view – true cuts in cost should release money for other, more worthy social projects, but to simplify the expenditure as simply an observation on the level of civilisation was reactionary at best. A number of the shipyard workers had entered into a scheme known locally as 'the establishment', basically a form of pensions contribution. The scheme had worked extremely well for a great number of years, indeed, 'during the whole period over which this system has been in operation we have never had what I may call labour troubles in our dockyards,' noted Liberal MP for Portsmouth Sir Thomas Bramsdon. The problem was, in an attempt to identify savings, one of the first things to go was 'the establishment'; closure of the scheme to those eligible had, over three years, ensured 800 skilled men had been denied this valuable incentive. Further, the cost of building the dreadnoughts should be seen as inward investment:

John Rees (Liberal)
How can this expenditure be other than productive? You spend about £2,000,000 sterling on every capital ship built. Seventy-five per cent, of the outlay is on British labour and British materials, and you employ from 1,500 to 2,000 men continuously in this island. Is not that just exactly what we want to do? How can it be held that the time when shipbuilding is rife, when the Government defences are being well looked after, that that is a period characterised by decay and decadence? Is it not notorious that during the whole period when Germany was building up her great armaments she was at the same time building up her industrial greatness even at a faster rate?
HC Deb 03 August 1909 vol. 8 cc1711-804

Rees was an ardent supporter of the drive to develop the navy and took a pragmatic approach to the situation of defence over welfare.

We hear that the Revenue about to be raised is to be devoted to social reforms and to defence, and there seems to be a perpetual struggle between these objects as to which should get the larger share, naval and military defence or social reform; but if our defences are not sufficient there will be no occasion for social reform.
HC Deb 03 August 1909 vol. 8 cc1711-804

Social welfare and reform aside, it was clear the government intended to construct four dreadnoughts whilst making provision for a further four in the near future. No sooner had the debate over 'eight' subsided than it was time to set the Estimates for 1910/11; the budget was huge. First Lord of the Admiralty McKenna opened the debate at 4 p.m. stating, 'No man who stands at this table can present Estimates of such a gigantic total as £40,600,000, without a very serious sense of responsibility.' Six hours later, McKenna called for a close of the day's business, drained from the discussion – especially a bad-tempered exchange with Lord Charles Beresford. It was time to regroup. A level of the intricacies demanded can be gauged from the section of debate below.

Dr Thomas Macnamara, Parliamentary and Financial Secretary to the Admiralty (Liberal)
We have in this programme five battleships, and the Noble Lord in the course of his speech seemed to think that was insufficient. At the London Chamber of Commerce he said:— I want ten battleships by the 31st March, 1914, and if the contingent four battleships are laid down I want six. The four vessels have been laid down, and they are no longer contingent. Therefore the Noble Lord only wants six.

Lord Charles Beresford (Conservative)
Read on. I said that is not subject to any German acceleration, in which case I wanted ten. I wanted six this year, six next year, and the four that ought to have been built last year. We are one short of what I wanted.

Lord Charles Beresford.

Macnamara. I will read it from the Noble Lord's programme:— My programme is as follows: Ten battleships – I put battleships, they are what are called 'Dreadnoughts'. In that ten is included the four which the country is asking for now when they ask for eight, the Government have now suggested four. If they put down eight I only want six. If they do not put down eight I want ten. That is all. We put the four down and there are only six left. There are two programmes to get that in – 1910-11, 1911-12 – so that the Noble Lord's programme would be secured by laying three down each year. We have got five in one year and he is not satisfied.

Beresford. Oh, no.

HC Deb 14 March 1910 vol. 15 cc38-147

Whilst all the bluster of the Navy Scare had been discussed through Parliament and the newspapers, some attempts were being made to slow the arms race. The key point was an attempt to offset the huge expenditure capital ships construction demanded. David Lloyd George had met the German Ambassador to London in July 1908 to discuss the financial implications for both countries. The talks went well, but when the Kaiser learnt of the topic, he was not happy: 'No there will be no talk about that at all!' he noted. When the third and fourth keels of the Royal Navy's first four confirmed dreadnoughts were laid down in July 1909, it was clear the British intended to maintain their superiority. On 21 August, the German Chancellor, Theobald von Bethmann-Hollweg, informed the British Embassy in Berlin of the intention to open talks on the subject. They came to nothing; German public opinion alone would not be favourable, and even if this could be won round, the possibility of repealing the Navy Law was nonexistent. What did come out of the sessions was a slight slowing of production and an agreement, by July 1911, to share technical information – up to a point.

Agadir

That point was reached on 1 July 1911 when the German gunboat SMS *Panther* steamed into Agadir harbour under the ruse of protection for German Industrialists. Morocco had been assured of its sovereign independence by the beginning of the twentieth century; however, France considered itself the primary political force in the area and had troops stationed across the country. Crucially, this view was supported by Britain. Germany also had a stake in the country, obtaining an open trade agreement that allowed her to have some commercial rights to mineral deposits. Convoluted discussion ensued, complicated by the overthrow of the Sultan by his brother, but finally, by 1909, agreement was reached. A bilateral treaty with both France and Germany agreeing to respect the rights of the other was signed in February. The treaty failed, France continued to exert political pressure on the north of the country and threatened to back it up with military force, suggesting Europeans could be in danger. Berlin took the opportunity to do the same in the south, but with no ground troops in the vicinity, elected to use navy ships as a show of strength.

Four days after the *Panther* dropped anchor, the light cruiser SMS *Berlin* arrived and manoeuvres with the Royal Navy were cancelled. The French Government was incensed. There was no way the Germans would be allowed to partition Morocco – public opinion alone would not allow it. Interestingly, no one had considered Britain's stance on the situation. British trade in the country was bigger than the Germans', so partition between the two European countries would be unthinkable; however, more dangerous was the renewed relationship with the French people – the *Entente Cordiale*. The matter was raised in the Commons:

> Mr Balfour, Perhaps the Prime Minister will redeem his promise and carry out what he led the House to believe he would be able to do today, that is make a statement to the House as to the present affairs in Morocco?

> The Prime Minister (Asquith)
> Recent events are causing discussions between the Powers most interested in Morocco, and at this stage I can say little of the negotiations which are passing between them. But I wish it clearly understood that His Majesty's Government consider that a new

SMS *Panther*. Her arrival in Agadir harbour caused talk of war.

situation has arisen in Morocco in which it is possible that future developments may affect British interests more directly that has hitherto been the case. I am confident that diplomatic discussion will find a solution, and in the part that we shall take in it we shall have due regard to the protection of those interests and to the fulfilment of our treaty obligations to France, which are well known to the House.

HC Deb 06 July 1911 vol. 27 c1341

The world waited whilst the German Government planned its next move, the possibility of war on many lips. By 21 July, the Foreign Secretary Grey had requested a meeting with the German Ambassador to demand answers – none were forthcoming, forcing British frustration to boil over in the most unlikely of places. That evening, at the Mansion House, David Lloyd George, often considered to be pro-German, let loose a speech that left Berlin in no doubt as to where the British Government stood on the matter. In forcefully underpinning Britain's desire to stay a world power, Lloyd George had demonstrated to the world that they would back any French claims; Berlin's position looked untenable, surely they would withdraw from the Moroccan coast. They did not – conflict looked increasingly likely. Winston Churchill, then Home Secretary, took it upon himself to prepare the nation for enemy sabotage at naval ports, whilst in Germany the implications of an armed struggle with Britain were deliberated. Above all else, the world now knew that the British would stand by France if they were pushed into conflict with Germany; the *Entente Cordiale* looked increasingly solid. Talks dragged on into the autumn with an agreement, considered by many as a defeat for Germany, finally reached on 11 October 1911. One thing that did emerge from the crisis was the replacement of the First Lord of the Admiralty – the post would now be held by the formidable Winston Churchill.

'Winny'

It had become increasingly obvious that whilst McKenna had been generally receptive to the demands of the Navy, he had not been committed enough to follow through some radical changes. Agadir demonstrated that, if war did break out in Europe, Germany would take, if not instigate, a major move on the territorial acquisitions of others. Even if this did not directly involve British territories, it was likely to affect the trade routes. With this in mind, the government recognised a dynamic First Lord of the Admiralty was required; Asquith approached Churchill whilst both were in Scotland; on Monday 25 October 1911, Churchill took up office at the Admiralty. He was a decision maker of the first order. A number of major items from the 1911 Navy Estimates had yet to be provisioned; Churchill immediately placed orders for twenty destroyers with manufacturers. He appointed Rear Admiral Sir David Beatty as the Private Naval Secretary, eventually guiding him through to command of the Battle Cruiser Squadrons before taking command of the Grand Fleet. He also contacted the retired Fisher, inviting him to comment and advise when and where necessary; Lord Fisher was immediately on call. One of his first pieces of advice was to prepare for

Winston Churchill in 1914.

war in mid-1914. Intuitively, Fisher estimated that by July/August, the Germans would have completed the Kiel Canal and the way would be open to conflict.

Of all Churchill's achievements at the Admiralty before the outbreak of war, the introduction of the Queen Elizabeth class must rank the highest. They were monsters along side of the original *Dreadnought*, inevitably gaining the title Super-Dreadnoughts. Armament was exceptional: eight 15-inch guns were the main weapon, able to destroy targets at ranges in excess of eleven miles. Even with a displacement of 34,500 tons fully laden, they could still achieve 24 knots, and that speed was provided by Parsons direct-drive steam turbines through four shafts, boilers crucially fired by oil instead of coal. The move to oil had been mused for a number of years by the Royal Navy; indeed, it was already in service with the submarine force and a number of destroyers were using it, whilst the United States Navy were also in the process of building two battleships to be powered by oil. Many argued that Britain ran on coal – it had, for 200 years, fired the industrial revolution and allowed her to build an Empire; now the First Lord of the Admiralty wanted to place the entire motive power of the Royal Navy in the hands of an imported material.

An extensive inquiry into oil by Lord Fisher, requested by Churchill, concluded the advantages far outweighed any perceived problems, especially if a war reserve was stockpiled. Coaling was a dirty, time-consuming job with everyone becoming embroiled in either shovelling it or dragging sacks around the ship. As we will see later, coal became the deciding factor in the Battle of the Falklands in the first months of the war. To ensure an adequate war reserve was quickly built up, the government gained a controlling interest in the Anglo-Persian Oil Company, currently opening up vast areas of Arabia, by investing capital in return for a secure supply. Unfortunately, only a few ships were to benefit from this innovation before the outbreak of war.

Holidays

Agadir, although seen as a slap in the face for the German Government, gave Tirpitz the opportunity to move away from 'Risk' and realign his expansion programme. He suggested that the Imperial Navy should aim for a 2:3 ratio completed by 1918; to achieve this he would need a dreadnought construction tally of three per year on top of those already in production. By the time Churchill was aware of this, it was too late to incorporate any response into the 1911/12 Estimates. Naturally, relations already strained by the Moroccan incident were further aggravated by the revelations, concerning London so much they sent a special delegation to discuss the growing rift. Under the guise of visiting technical education centres, Richard Haldane, current Minister for War, opened a dialogue exploring the possibility of an arms limitation 'agreement' of some sort. His message to Tirpitz and the Kaiser was simple – continue to increase the number of battleships and Britain would have no option but to expand alongside. Haldane came away with very little; construction would be slowed by one ship but only for one year, then production would follow the original pattern. Tirpitz would still request, and get, funding for the required number of vessels to form a third battle squadron, it would just take an extra year to complete. Interestingly, the Kaiser gave Haldane a copy of the proposed new Navy Bill and suggested he showed it to the Admiralty. Churchill, once the document had been fully translated, went into overdrive! When the First Lord of the Admiralty spoke in the Cabinet Office on 14 February 1911, it was to inform the ministers of a grave fact. It transpired that Germany's preparation was, in everything but name, aimed at a war with the United Kingdom. If nothing could be done to persuade Tirpitz to make his six-year programme a twelve-year one, the only option open would be to increase the number of British ships. Speaking in Glasgow on 9 February, Churchill, in true style, described the Royal Navy as a purely defensive required because of Britain's island status. Germany, on the other hand needed a strong army but the navy was no more than a luxury!

It was time for desperate measures – someone would have to convince the German Government that their relentless building programme was taking them down a ruinous path. Proposals put forward by London talked of a non-aggressive policy towards Germany and no outright intention to attack her. Unfortunately, this did not go far enough for the Kaiser. In an attempt to split the *Entente Cordiale*, Berlin required a fixed neutrality clause – in essence Britain was to re-enter a state of 'Splendid Isolation'. Besides, the German press were outranged at Churchill's claim that the Imperial Fleet was no more than a whim – the talks collapsed before they really got going. What was needed was a novel approach. During the Navy Estimates speech to the House on 18 March 1912, Churchill described what he had in mind:

> If Germany elected to drop out any one or even any two, of these annual quotas and to put the money into her pocket for the enjoyment of her people ... we will at once ... blot out our corresponding quota.

The time had come to discuss openly the great financial commitment both countries were making in the pursuit of domination over the other. With reform and other social welfare initiatives still being developed, any reduction in the relentlessly escalating costs of the Royal Navy would be welcome respite. Churchill wagered if he could demonstrate a major financial incentive to slow arms production, Berlin might just take notice:

> Take – the year 1913. In that year, as I apprehend, Germany will build three capital ships, and it will be necessary for us to build five in consequence. Suppose we were both to take a 'holiday' for that year. Supposing we both introduced a blank page in the book of misunderstanding; suppose that Germany were to build no ships in that year, she would save herself between £6 million and £7 million sterling. But that is not all. We would not in ordinary circumstances begin our ships until she has started hers. The three ships that she did not build would therefore automatically wipe out no fewer than five British potential super-dreadnoughts, and that is more than I expect them to hope to do in a brilliant naval action.
>
> HC Deb 26 March 1913 vol. 50 cc1749-800

The offer was ignored. After all, was not the German Fleet no more than a luxury?

Mediterranean Drawdown

Tensions were now such that any movement of troops or naval assets caused a flurry of diplomatic interest. So, when the Royal Navy finally began removing ships stationed in Malta, Berlin reacted badly. Especially as the French Navy began to move parts of its Atlantic Fleet into the Mediterranean just after six older battleships had sailed for the United Kingdom. No agreement stood between the two neighbours, but from the outside, the rearrangement of forces in the region looked just a little suspicious. Berlin began to feel very isolated. In reality, the drawdown was just another part of Fisher's plan to be strong in the areas that mattered. He had already closed a number of stations around the world – Churchill was just continuing this policy, replacing old with new whilst taking the opportunity to redeploy experienced sailors to the dreadnoughts. It was hoped that by 1915 the Royal Navy would be of a size that would allow the redeployment of a number of battleships to the Mediterranean. Until then, the primary concern – remember Churchill was familiar with the actual Navy Law passed through the Reichstag – was the protection of Britain and clear water in the North Sea.

When the First Lord of the Admiralty stood up to deliver the Navy Estimates speech on 26 March 1913, he again talked of savings for the public purse. The increased number of personnel now needed to operate the expanding fleet had alone pushed up annual costs by £730,000; this was further exacerbated by the relentless march of technology. It was not just the construction cost of new ships that worried the Treasury; a further £1,500,000 increase could be attributed to the development of the Royal Naval Air Service and the incorporation of wireless both onboard and on a network of land stations around the globe. But most telling of all, especially for Berlin,

> The Estimates of this year would, indeed, have been substantially higher but for the extreme congestion in the shipyards arising from the extraordinary demands upon

our shipbuilding plant, and especially upon our skilled labour supply, which are the characteristics of the present moment.

Mr Churchill's Statement
HC Deb 26 March 1913 vol. 50 cc1749-800

The conditions predicted by Tirpitz some years earlier had been freely admitted in the House of Commons. The German push for a ratio of 2:3, with the Imperial Navy having sixty dreadnought-class ships, gambling British manufacturing capability would not be able to construct ninety in response had been accurate. Clearly, the 'holiday' Churchill again asked for was more in response to overstretched manufacturers rather than the German public purse. In a suitable response, Berlin noted that, if she conformed to the principles of a 'holiday', much of the skilled workforce might well travel to France or Russia to build ships. The likelihood was that the German yards would not be able to re-employ them once the 'holiday' was over and Britain would consequently hold the advantage once construction restarted. There would be no holiday.

Beginning of the End

Then, in April 1914, German suspicions were confirmed: the United Kingdom appeared to be pursuing a policy of encirclement. Their apparent agreement with France – outwardly appearing to have a major military element concerning the Mediterranean – was concern enough. Now, after an extended period of trying to impose arms reductions on Berlin unsuccessfully, she was trying to encircle her. It was true St Petersburg had been trying to open talks with London since 1908, primarily because she had yet to recover from the monumental losses inflicted by the Japanese. The Tsar had also jealously eyed the *Entente Cordiale*, hoping something similar could be brokered between Russia and Britain. Foreign Secretary Grey finally relented to exploratory talks conducted in secret; outwardly, nothing was discussed. Once Berlin knew the talks were underway, they were made public via the German media, a sure-fire way of disrupting them. The talks came to nothing but the damage had been done. Britain, despite its offers of non-aggression towards Germany, clearly intended to encircle her. Outwardly, both nations sought to dispel any alarm but events were already in train. On 23 June 1914, the Second Battle Squadron of the Royal Navy entered Kiel Harbour, attending, by invitation, the Regatta. Further up the coast, the First Battle Cruiser Squadron entered Kronstadt, the Russian naval port. Five days of hosted visits across Germany greeted the British crews, spreading them as far as Berlin. Of course, some decided the only reason the Royal Navy was at the regatta was to spy on the preparedness of the Imperial Navy in readiness for war; a charge countered by the Royal Navy giving almost unrestricted access to all British ships. However, the mood was dampened on 28 June when the Kaiser received word of the death of his friend in Sarajevo. He promptly left Kiel to prepare for the funeral, only to be advised not to travel due to fears for his safety. Leaving on 30 June, Vice-Admiral Sir George Warrender had his squadron radio 'Friends in past and friends forever'. Just over a month later, both navies would be adversaries in the greatest armed struggle the world had seen.

Four

The Greatest Catastrophe

Mr Bonar Law (Conservative)
May I ask the Prime Minister if he has any information he can give us to-day?

The Prime Minister (Asquith)
Our Ambassador at Berlin received his passports at seven o'clock last evening and since eleven o'clock last night a state of war has existed between Germany and ourselves.

HC Deb 05 August 1914 vol. 65 cc1963-4 1963

With that simple statement in the House of Commons, Britain was plunged into the costliest war to date. For days, the German Government had been demanding routes through neutral Belgium's countryside. Brussels had rejected the requests as unacceptable within international law, and war with Britain became a real possibility. On the morning of 4 August 1914, the British Minister in Brussels telegrammed London with bad news:

> German Minister has this morning addressed Note to the Belgian Minister for Foreign Affairs stating that as Belgian Government have declined the well-intended proposals submitted to them by the Imperial Government, the latter will, deeply to their regret, be compelled to carry out, if necessary by force of arms, the measures considered indispensable in view of the French menaces.

The oncoming storm had been gathering pace since 28 June 1914 and continued to do so across the Continent, steadily subsuming all the major powers of Europe, primarily through agreements and treaties rather that direct acts of violence.

What brought about this monumental tide of destruction can be traced to an ill-conceived royal visit by Archduke Franz Ferdinand, heir to the Austrian throne, to the provinces of Bosnia and Herzegovina. An attack was planned by a Serbian nationalist group known locally as Black Hand, who had, since 1911, been campaigning for rights within the provinces. In the event, it was a handful of Bosnians who finally decided violence was the only course of action. On 28 June 1914, the Archduke and his wife toured Sarajevo, and after a disastrous attempt to throw a grenade into the car they were travelling in, one of the Bosnian terrorists, nineteen-year-old Gavrilo Princip, managed to get close enough to shoot both the royal occupants. News of the assassinations made the following day's Commons sitting in London. The Prime Minister, Herbert Asquith announced,

> I beg to give notice that I shall to-morrow move that a humble address be presented to His Majesty expressing the sentiments of this House on the assassination of His Imperial Royal Highness the Archduke Francis Ferdinand of Austria, and his Consort.
>
> HC Deb 29 June 1914 vol. 64 c53 53

The assassination gave the Austrian government the excuse it needed to begin military action against Serbia; however, it took nearly three weeks before an official reaction was published. Initially, this was interpreted as the nation being in mourning for the Archduke; in reality, Austria was eager to ensure they had German support for any military action. On 5 July, Count Hoyos, an Austrian diplomat, delivered a letter to Berlin explaining,

> The Sarajevo affair was not merely the bloody deed of a single individual, but was the result of a well organised conspiracy, the threads of which can be traced to Belgrade; and even though it will probably prove impossible to get evidence of the complicity of the Serbian Government, there can be no doubt that its policy, directed towards the unification of all the Southern-Slav countries under the Serbian flag, is responsible for such crimes, and that the continuation of such a state of affairs constitutes an enduring peril for my house and my possessions.

Archduke Francis Ferdinand of Austria and his Consort.

On 23 July, Austria issued Serbia an ultimatum demanding the assassins be brought to justice: all anti-Austrian officials in government should be expelled, no more anti-Austrian lessons in Serbian schools and a number of prominent Serbian officials should be arrested and tried over the murders. Serbia looked to its alliance with Russia as a means of protecting itself, an assurance given on 25 July should Serbia be attacked. That same day, the Serbian Government accepted all but one point in the ultimatum, hoping to buy some time; it failed, and that afternoon, the vast Austro-Hungarian Empire mobilised. London launched a last-ditch diplomatic initiative, hoping to draw in Germany, Italy and France; however, Sir E. Grey, the Secretary of State for Foreign Affairs, duly noted,

> It must be obvious to any person who-reflects upon the situation that the moment the dispute ceases to be one between Austria-Hungary and Serbia and becomes one in which another Great Power is involved, it can but end in the greatest catastrophe that has ever befallen the Continent of Europe at one blow: no one can say what would be the limit of the issues that might be raised by such a conflict, the consequences of it, direct and; indirect would be incalculable.
>
> HC Deb 27 July 1914 vol. 65 cc936-9

The Austro-Hungarian Government officially declared war on Serbia on 28 July, bombarding Belgrade and forcing the Russians, bound by treaty, to mobilise against Austria and Germany. By 1 August, France and Germany had mobilised and Berlin had declared war on Russia. Germany now demanded passage through Belgium, having invaded Luxembourg the previous day in an attempt to reach Paris quickly; Brussels denied them. Germany declared war on France on 3 August, invading neutral Belgium the following day. Britain, holding up the 1839 neutrality agreement with Belgium, declared war on Germany the same day. By the end of the month, the majority of Northern Europe, save Italy, had become embroiled in the 'greatest catastrophe'.

So, can we recognise a train of events that bring the German High Seas Fleet to the East Coast on the morning of 16 December 1914? It appears that even with the preceding arms race and realignment of naval strength around the globe, Tirpitz's risk theory continued to by played out. From the outset, the Royal Navy had been expecting a major showdown with the High Seas Fleet in the North Sea. All indications were that the new German battle fleet was constructed for just such a venture; conditions on board were cramped with crew necessities, e.g., washrooms, laundries, mess decks, in sparse supply. This assumption had forced the Admiralty to keep a large number of ships in readiness around the British coast. That containment concentrated a vast amount of shipping in a small geographical area. However, the road to Scarborough covers the globe and subsequently major engagements in the Indian Ocean and waters around South America need to be considered. This includes the larger naval chess game being played out between the British and German Admiralty that ultimately gave the High Seas Fleet their window of opportunity. Indeed, the North Sea had not yet seen a major engagement but that was about to change thanks to a relatively new weapons system – the submarine.

German troops were quick to act; as they invaded neutral Belgium, Britain was forced to declare war.

A detachment of German sailors in Brussels.

'Three before Breakfast'

At first light on 22 September 1914, submarine U-9, captained by Lt Otto Weddigen, spotted three British ships of the Seventh Cruiser Squadron steaming in line. Less than two hours later, all three armoured cruisers, sixty-two officers and over 1,400 men had been sent to the bottom. The action caused outrage in Britain, but more importantly, it demonstrated the effectiveness of submarines in warfare and changed Royal Naval tactics forever.

The Seventh Cruiser Squadron formed part of the Third Fleet of the Home Fleets, lying in reserve on the South Coast since May 1912. Creation of the Third Fleet had been 'Jackie' Fisher's answer to the skills gaps he had encountered when taking over as

Celebratory postcard
depicting the deeds of
German submarine U-9.

First Sea Lord in 1904. The Seventh Cruiser Squadron comprised the *Cressy*, *Aboukir*, *Bacchante*, *Euryalus* and *Hogue*, five of the six *Cressy*-class armoured cruisers laid down at the turn of the century. They were considered out of date by the outbreak of war; indeed, concern was such that requests were made to withdraw them from patrol duties if at all possible. A number of factors made them vulnerable. Crews on the ships had been retained at a nucleus level, ensuring only essential maintenance was undertaken and that the ships could be brought quickly to a war footing if required. When the call came, each ship's complement increased with inexperienced cadets, new recruits and reservists. Whenever possible, destroyers of the Harwich Force supported the cruisers but more often than not the weather ensured they patrolled alone. Most critically, however, the ships' propulsion had not stood the test of time. Originally designed for 21 knots, more often than not engine and boiler problems ensured 12 knots was the norm.

In August 1914, the Second and Third Fleets were combined to form the Channel Fleet, and in so doing, the *Aboukir*, *Cressy* and *Hogue* were re-stationed on the East Coast. Their primary task was now to protect the steady flow of merchantmen supplying Britain with essential imports. Concerns continued to be voiced throughout August and September over the ships' condition and capability to meet the enemy, so much so that those serving on board affectionately referred to them as the 'Live Bait Squadron'. And so it was that, on 22 September, the squadron was under the watchful eye of Otto Weddigen from the U-9.

With no destroyer escorts, lookouts were posted on all sides, scanning the sea for the tell-tail signs of a periscope or smoke over the horizon and a number of guns were at the ready. Weddigen crept in and fired one torpedo at HMS *Aboukir*; when it struck, it so damaged the structural integrity of her that the ship was gone in under twenty minutes. Seeing no assailant and deciding a mine was the culprit, both the *Cressy* and *Hogue* turned in to assist those crew now in the water, standing by to rescue any further ones who made it off the *Aboukir*. This time-honoured practice of coming to the aid of stricken ships, a tradition over 300 years old, proved the downfall of both. Weddigen could hardly believe his luck; two stationary targets now presented themselves to the U-9. Two torpedoes struck *Hogue*, again causing fatal damage, and with that the *Cressy*, realising it must be a submarine attack, got underway, but it was too late; two torpedoes finished her as well. One of the *Cressy*'s crew later recounted the event to reporters:

> The three vessels had been scouting, he said. A slight mist obscured the view. Suddenly the *Aboukir* was seen to keel over heavily. All hands on the *Cressy* were called, and this cruiser stood by to render assistance. The *Hogue*, also coming up, arrived first. Just as she was swinging her small boats over she seemed to be lifted clear of the water. By this time the *Aboukir* had gone down, and the water around her was filled with wreckage and swimming men.
>
> Just as the *Hogue* settled back in the water, the watchers on the *Cressy* caught a glimpse of a submarine. The *Cressy* immediately fired at it. The submarine disappeared, supposedly hit.
>
> Then our decks rippled beneath our feet! Said the midshipman, but the good old tub recovered her balance and would have staid up if we had not been torpedoed a second time. She rolled over so slowly that we had plenty of time to jump well clear of the ship before she disappeared beneath the water. Then it was swim for your life. I was picked up by the cruiser *Lowestoft*.
>
> *The New York Times*, 23 September 1914

The loss of three ships was downplayed publicly. The Admiralty releasing a statement to the press on 25 September noting the class was already obsolete and once they had ceased to be cost effective would be scrapped. However, the rapid technological advancements in submarine warfare made it necessary for some of the more pleasant and honourable aspects of naval operations to be abandoned. The practice of standing by to pick up survivors was to be abandoned in favour of saving the ship.

Above left: HMS *Cressy*.

Above right: The end of the 'live bait' squadron.

Modern naval warfare is presenting us with so many new and strange situations that an error of judgment of this character is pardonable. But it has been necessary to point out for the further guidance of his Majesty's ships that conditions which prevail when a vessel of a squadron is injured in a mine field, or is subjected to submarine attack, are analogous to those which occur in action, and that the rule of leaving disabled ships to their own resources is applicable, so far, at any rate, as large vessels are concerned.

Admiralty Press Statement, 25 September 1914

Irrespective of the shift in operations when considered under attack, it was now clear that 'traditional' surface actions were a thing of the past. Combating submarine warfare required a major shift in tactical thinking, for in just over an hour, one submarine had sunk three large Royal Navy vessels and in so doing caused the biggest loss of life at sea in three generations. Such was the indignation, early reports noted at least three U-boats were involved and that the *Cressy* had sunk two of them. When it was revealed that a single submarine was involved, public opinion hardened considerably against the Germans and their clearly underhanded way of conducting war on the high sea.

The South Atlantic

Whilst the tragedy in the North Sea was unfolding, a further, more critical one was developing in waters around South America. During the early part of the war, the British had captured a number of Germany's eastern colonies. These included Samoa and around one-third of Papua New Guinea, then named Kaiser Wilhelmsland, both of which had been quickly overrun by Australian troops.

The German East Asia Squadron

The German East Asia Squadron was the Kaiser's only true deep-water formation at that time that operated independently of the High Seas Fleet. The squadron was based at Tsingtao on the Chinese coast, a legacy of the rush to acquire ports in China, until the outbreak of war when, fearing attacks from the Japanese and Australian navies, Vice-Admiral Count Maximilian von Spee, set sail for the Pacific. Maximilian Graf von Spee was born on 22 June 1861 in Copenhagen, the son of a prominent Rhenish family. He joined the Imperial German Navy in 1878, becoming the commander of ports in German West Africa ten years later. Von Spee was appointed Chief of Staff of the North Sea Command in 1908, becoming Rear Admiral two years later. In 1912, he took command of the now ill-fated German East Asia Squadron, becoming Vice-Admiral that same year.

The squadron comprised two armoured cruisers, SMS *Scharnhorst* and SMS *Gneisenau*, complemented by light cruisers SMS *Leipzig*, *Dresden* and *Nürnberg*. A number of support vessels, including colliers, also followed the squadron around the coast, supplying the ships' incessant demands for coal. One further light cruiser, the SMS *Emden*, was deployed into the Indian Ocean as a commerce raider, causing major headaches for the Allies. She

Above left: Vice-Admiral Count Maximillian von Spee.

Above right: Dresden memorial on Juan Fernandez island. (C. McCutcheon)

operated in an area of trade interests critical to the British economy, including routes from Ceylon, India, New Zealand, Australia and the Far East, a situation further complicated by the huge amount of troops currently shipping through the area en route to Europe, giving the *Emden* the potential to cause great loss of life. The *Emden*'s crew became very efficient raiders, claiming twenty-one cargos as prize and sinking a large number of Allied merchant shipping. Indeed, no tea was sailed from ports in Ceylon between 4 September and 7 October due to the *Emden* threat. On the night of 22 September, the *Emden* shelled the Burmah Oil Company's oil storage installation at Madras on the East Coast of India. She also damaged a large number of ships docked in the port before slipping away prior the coastal batteries engaging her. Time and again, the *Emden* seemed to be one step ahead of her would-be attackers, forcing the Allies to commit more ships to the search for her.

On 9 November, the *Emden* arrived at Direction Island, a component of the Cocos (Keeling) Islands in the Indian Ocean. Situated on the island was a radio station operated by the Eastern Telegraph Company, the destruction of which would have a major impact on military communications throughout the region. In an attempt to save valuable ammunition, the captain decided to put a demolition crew together and destroy the station by hand rather than shell it. Unfortunately for the *Emden*, as she had approached the island, a general warning to shipping was issued by the wireless station staff. This alerted a number of patrolling Allied ships to the impending attack and within the day, the Australian light cruiser HMAS *Sydney* had been relieved of escort duties and was in sight of the island. Catching the *Emden* unawares, the *Sydney* proceeded to shell the German ship for over an hour, inflicting major damage and forcing her crew to beach her. Ignoring demands to surrender, the *Sydney* blasted the stricken vessel at close quarters, wrecking her in the process.

The end of the *Emden* has some implications for our current investigations. Clearly, the crew of the *Emden* considered destroying the wireless station at Direction Island

Above left: SMS *Emden* caused havoc across the Indian Ocean.

Above right: The wreck of the *Emden* at Direction Island.

by hand a worthwhile risk; had she shelled the station, she would have slipped away before the *Sydney* arrived. The importance of wireless stations during the war cannot be underestimated. Both Scarborough and Whitby had radio stations; both were targeted. The reliance on radio is further underpinned when we consider the story of the rest of Vice-Admiral von Spee's East Asia Squadron.

Coronel

Whilst the *Emden* had been successfully causing havoc, von Spee was assembling the rest of the dispersed East Asia Fleet ready for the long haul back to Germany. The only problem was the *Emden* had been so successful that the Pacific was now teeming with British and Allied naval shipping, and whilst the *Emden* had been destroyed, it was well known the Germans' second strongest naval element was still at large. The path of least resistance, von Spee wagered, would be round Cape Hope and through the South Atlantic. He needed to build a network of safe ports and coaling points along the way, but Berlin had assured the Vice-Admiral this would be no problem. The route would entail passing the British-owned Falkland Islands but reports suggested these were next to abandoned and subsequently posed no threat. The finalised plan required the squadron to sail down the west coast of South America, calling in at Easter Island for the pre-Cape leg of the voyage whilst taking advantage of any enemy trading vessels along the way.

    The closest British force was the squadron commanded by Rear Admiral Christopher Cradock, comprising a fleet of predominantly elderly armoured and light cruisers. Sir Christopher George Francis Maurice Cradock had joined the Royal Navy in 1875. He saw action in the Mediterranean and during Boxer Rebellion, where he commanded a multi-national force during the capture of the Taku forts; he was awarded the Prussian Order of the

Above: SMS *Scharnhorst*, *Gneisenau* and *Nürnberg* prepare to leave the Chilean port of Valparaiso on 4 November.

Right: Rear Admiral Christopher Cradock.

Crown as a direct result. Promoted to Rear Admiral in 1910, Cradock was awarded the KCVO in 1912 and took command of the North America and West Indies Stations the following year.

He had been steadily working his way down the East Coast of South America from the Caribbean in search of commerce raiders and German cargo. Signals intercepted by the Admiralty and ships across the Pacific Ocean were now indicating von Spee would, in all probability, take a route around the Cape in an attempt to get to the Atlantic. Cradock was signalled to that effect on 14 September and ordered to meet the largest of the East Asia Squadron, the armoured cruisers SMS *Scharnhorst* and SMS *Gneisenau*, with matching force, should the need arise. For von Spee to have any chance of success, he would need to assemble the squadron and make a final coaling stop near Easter Island before the dash either around the Cape or through the Magellan Straits. Either way, the chances were they would encounter British forces.

To assist Cradock, the Admiralty dispatched HMS *Defence* from duties in the Mediterranean and HMS *Canopus*, an elderly, pre-dreadnought battleship from the Canary Islands. *Canopus* had been at the Canary Islands station since 21 August in support of a cruiser squadron, and as part of the beefing up of naval stations around the world. As the possibility of action around South America became more likely, she was dispatched to Abrolhos Rock, off the coast of Brazil, arriving there on 22 September. That same day, *Scharnhorst* and *Gneisenau* entered the French Polynesian port of Papeete in an attempt to take advantage of coal stocks but the port staff fired the piles before they had chance. Two ships were sunk including a French gunboat the *Zélée* and the impounded German freighter *Walkure* before the cruisers bombarded the town using precious ammunition in the process. The bombardment indicated that von Spee was heading for the South American coast and now clearly intended to round the Cape.

Above left: SMS *Scharnhorst.*

Above right: SMS *Dresden.*

The events around the South American coast were to claim a victim in London as well. The First Sea Lord, Prince Louis of Battenberg, had held the post since replacing Admiral Sir Francis Bridgeman in December 1912. He was the third to fill the position since Fisher had left in 1910 – all three were charged in the press with having a weak attitude, effectively allowing the drive Fisher had instilled in the service to wane. Naturally, the outbreak of war stirred up anti-German sentiment; it was not long before a combination of pressure from the press and a number of members of Parliament forced Battenberg – with his obvious German connections – to resign on advice from Churchill on 28 October 1914. The indomitable Lord Fisher replaced him.

On the morning of 30 October, 'Jackie' Fisher was back at the Admiralty. Reoccupying the position of First Sea Lord, his first task was to reassess the navy's position. Churchill immediately briefed him the moment he entered the building. Over a two-hour session, Fisher was brought rapidly up to speed on the Royal Navy's current world commitment. It was clear a major situation was developing around the coast of South America and Churchill, already well aware of the *Canopus'* shortcomings and Cradock's orders, asked,

> Speaking of Admiral Cradock's position, I said, 'You don't suppose he would try to fight them without the *Canopus?'*
>
> He [Fisher] did not give any decided reply.

On 31 October, von Spee learnt, via a telegraph from the German supply vessel *Gottingen*, that HMS *Glasgow* had just entered the Chilean port of Coronel. She was in port to collect signals and messages from the British consulate in the town. During her voyage north, the *Glasgow* had picked up significant enemy radio traffic; identifying it as SMS *Leipzig*, she had informed Cradock. Cradock, with orders to intercept the German fleet, rounded the Cape and proceeded north up the coast of Chile, crucially leaving the slow *Canopus* behind to protect the Royal Naval colliers, as Churchill had

HMS *Canopus*.

Fisher and
Churchill
discuss the latest
developments at
the Admiralty.

feared. Von Spee, sensing an easy target, headed for Coronel, expecting to engage just
Glasgow; Cradock, for his part, expected only *Leipzig*. What Cradock did not know
was the von Spee had been using the *Leipzig* radio call sign as a cover for his entire
fleet; the Royal Navy was steaming towards overwhelming German superiority and
disaster.

The fleets made visual contact due west of Coronel on the afternoon of 1 November.
Cradock, whose flagship was HMS *Good Hope*, was accompanied by HMS *Monmouth*
and an armed merchantman, the *Otranto*; by now, the only heavy guns Cradock had
were 300 miles south of his current position escorting the colliers. The *Glasgow* quickly
formed up on the rest of the British ships and Cradock tried to engage the enemy
whilst the light was at his advantage. Realising this, von Spee resisted the temptation
until dusk, when the British fleet was silhouetted against the skyline. Within the hour,
the superior gunnery and targeting equipment on the more modern German ships had
sunk both the *Good Hope* and *Monmouth*, taking Cradock and over 1,600 crew with

them. The *Otranto* and *Glasgow* now steamed south to rendezvous with *Canopus*; radio jamming by the Germans meant she could not be warned immediately and, if not stopped, would also run into the overwhelming power of the East Asia Squadron. The action raised severe comments in the House of Lords a few days later:

Earl of Shelborne (Conservative)
All the cruisers on both sides concerned are over 20-knot cruisers – I think, running up to 22 and 23 knots. I do not suppose the *Canopus* at the most can steam more than 17-knots. Therefore, it was perfectly clear that so long as the *Good Hope* and *Monmouth* were in company with the *Canopus* they never by any possibility could force the German squadron to action. Consequently, for the purpose of catching and defeating the German squadron the addition of the *Canopus* to the cruisers we have lost was obviously futile.

I confess that the explanation about the *Canopus* only filled me with astonishment, and with a greater desire for an explanation from the Government as to how this could ever have come to pass. It is quite clear what happened. The *Good Hope* and the *Monmouth* and the *Glasgow* had to meet the whole of the German squadron alone, and from that moment it was only a contest between the two 9.2 guns of the *Good Hope* and the sixteen 8.2 guns of the *Scharnhorst* and the *Gneisenau*, and there could be no doubt whatever as to the issue.

HL Deb 11 November 1914 vol. 18 cc3-53

The loss of the *Monmouth* and *Good Hope* along with so many officers, crew and Rear Admiral Cradock forced London to drastically rethink its South Atlantic strategy. Sinking the cruisers had little effect on the overall Royal Navy strength; however, it was the first major loss in a surface battle for more than one hundred years. Also, coming so quickly on the heels of U-9's success in the North Sea, it was bound to damage Britain's 'rule the waves' image. For von Spee, the victory was to be short-lived. The newly reappointed First Sea Lord would see to that. The German squadron had placed itself in a precarious position. Coal was becoming ever more difficult to obtain, and the actions at Papeete and Coronel had used nearly half the ammunition reserves. However, it was to be the weather that finally drove von Spee's ships into the hands of the British, restored the Royal Navy's reputation and showed the German High Command that the time was right to strike in the North Sea.

Fisher, working on his pre-war premise that overwhelming force was the only way to ensure victory over any enemy – the entire reason he commissioned the Dreadnoughts – now set about rearranging the distribution of heavy ships south of the equator. His first act was to strip battle cruisers from the Grand Fleet. Two of those redeployed were the *Invincible* and *Inflexible*, both in dock at the time; Fisher expected them to sail with the dockworkers on board if the refits were not completed. By 11 November, both were underway – the work, unsurprisingly, completed ahead of schedule. A third battle cruiser, *Princess Royal*, was dispatched from the fleet and stationed off the East Coast of North America in case von Spee decided to run north through the Panama Canal. Further Royal Navy reorganisation demonstrates just how effective a major fleet loose in the southern oceans could be. A squadron of armoured cruisers were stationed in the West Indies,

HMS *Invincible*.

further complementing the *Princess Royal*. South Africa was also strengthened; HMS *Minotaur* on Indian Ocean convoy duties was detached to the Cape in support of HMS *Albion*. HMS *Defence*, en route to the South Atlantic, was also diverted to South Africa and complemented with an additional three light cruisers. A new squadron was formed on the West Coast of Africa in case von Spee took the opportunity to raid commerce in the area. Further ships were moved south from Canadian waters, and preparations were made to bring further elements of the Japanese fleet into the Pacific.

The man to command this assembling task force was to be Sir Frederick Charles Doveton Sturdee. Sturdee was born 9 June 1859 into a seagoing family; he received an education at the Royal Naval School before entered the service in July 1871. By the age of fourteen, he had made midshipman, serving in the Channel Squadron and the East India Station. Studying both gunnery and the new technology torpedoes, Sturdee went on to see service in the Mediterranean before returning to Portsmouth as a torpedo specialist. After a tour in Australia commanding HMS *Porpoise*, he returned to the Admiralty as assistant to the Director of Naval Intelligence and in 1902 was promoted to Chief Staff Officer of the Mediterranean Fleet. By 1906, Sturdee was back at sea on HMS *New Zealand*; however, on promotion to Rear Admiral in 1910, he took command of the First Battle Squadron of the Home Fleet. At the outbreak of war, he was Chief of War Staff at the Admiralty under the increasingly pilloried First Sea Lord, Prince Louis of Battenberg. Many saw Fisher's return as the end for Sturdee, but Churchill intervened, suggesting Sturdee might well demonstrate his courage at the head of the force to destroy von Spee.

On 26 November, von Spee set sail for the Cape and the subsequent run into the Atlantic. Almost immediately, they encountered a major storm that accompanied them for four days. All five ships were damaged but more importantly steaming into the storm had used nearly three times the usual amount of coal for the distance covered. Coal that was unlikely to be replaced once in the Atlantic, as Argentina and Brazil were not eager to supply German ships and the United States was steadily impounding vessels; a number of ocean liners were already incarcerated in New York. When the squadron rounded the Cape, they came upon a Canadian-owned steamer carrying 2,800 tons of finest Welsh steam coal. Unable to miss the windfall, von Spee spent the next three days re-coaling off the East Coast of the Picton Islands; the Royal Navy fleet were still four days from

Above: HMS *Inflexible* taking on board survivors from *Gneisenau.*

Left: Sir Frederick Charles Doveton Sturdee.

the Falkland Islands. Prior to sailing on 6 December, von Spee briefed his captains of the intention to attack the Falklands. All indications were that any enemy shipping was still two to three days away. *Canopus* and maybe *Glasgow* might be in the immediate area, but the islands should be relatively undefended. There was the opportunity to re-coal, destroy a key wireless station and maybe take the Governor captive.

The Admiralty also recognised the importance of the wireless station, considering it critical to the co-ordination of the destruction of the German squadron. Canopus had returned to the Falklands in mid-November where she was beached inside Stanley harbour to give protective fire over the southern approaches. Mines were laid across the harbour entrance and a local militia was raised in case the Germans planned to invade. Admiral Sturdee arrived at Stanley on 7 December and immediately began to coal, a process he hoped would be completed in two days. Unfortunately, the following morning, British lookouts spotted elements of the German squadron on the horizon; at this point, only HMS *Kent* was in any way ready for battle, the rest still completing coaling or needing several hours to raise a head of steam. *Gneisenau* and *Nürnberg* closed on the wireless station located on Wolf Rocks, and as they turned broadside to the installation, *Canopus* opened up at maximum elevation from within the harbour. Sensing larger ships present, the two Germans turned out of range, by which time *Inflexible* and *Invincible* closely followed by *Cornwall, Glasgow* and *Kent* had got underway. The day was clear, and it was not long before von Spee realised he had miscalculated the strength of the British Fleet, giving the order for the light cruisers to make good their escape.

Scharnhorst and *Gneisenau* then turned onto the enemy and prepared to accept action. The engagement with the *Inflexible* and *Invincible* lasted all afternoon. The Royal Navy fired the first shots at approximately 13.30; by 16.20 *Scharnhorst* was gone, and 1 hour 20 minutes later, *Gneisenau* suffered the same fate. Meanwhile, the cruisers were hunted down. The *Kent* sunk the *Nürnberg* at 19.27 whilst *Cornwall* and *Glasgow* had wrecked *Leipzig* – she sank at 21.23. The *Dresden* managed to escape but was later cornered off the coast of Chile in March 1915; she surrendered after a brief engagement. During the first 1915 sitting of the House of Lords, the Earl of Selborne observed,

> Turning to the battle off the Falkland Islands, there we have every reason to congratulate the Admiralty on the strategic conception which made that victory possible and the Admiral and his squadron on the mariner in which that victory was achieved. The Admiralty acted on one of Nelson's great maxims, that the best thing to do was to annihilate the enemy. I hope all our countrymen understand that so thoroughly was that maxim carried out that it is not going too far to say that Admiral Von Spee and his German squadron had no chance whatever, humanly speaking, against Admiral Sturdee and his British squadron, just as Admiral Cradock in his turn had no chance whatever with his squadron against Admiral Von Spee, and his squadron. The measure of Admiral Sturdee's success off the Falkland Islands is the measure of the blunder that the Admiralty made in furnishing Admiral Cradock with a squadron so wholly incompetent for the task that he was set to carry out in the Pacific. The moment has not yet come to follow that matter out either. We shall have to follow it out in time; but it is almost inconceivable that it should have been the same authority that armed Admiral Sturdee with his squadron and that armed Admiral Cradock with his squadron, both to perform the same task.
>
> HL Deb 07 January 1915 vol. 18 cc317-34

Naturally, the German press put on the best spin possible:

> That England needed an eightfold preponderance in fighting five German cruisers illustrates better than anything else that the English Admiralty fears the German Navy. We continue to trust in the efficiency of our bluejackets, and the pre-eminent ability of our naval leaders.
>
> *Koelnische Volks Zeitung*, 11 December 1914

One thing was now clear to both the Germans and British, the seas were free from German interference for the near future. Indeed, Churchill personally guaranteed this, proclaiming to the press, 'The peace of the Pacific is now, for the time being, assured.' However, regardless of the backslapping in the British newspapers, Parliamentary demands for an investigation into the tragedy of Admiral Cradock or the sheer belligerence of the German press, events off the coast of South America, including the search for the *Emden*, had weakened the strength of the Royal Navy in and around the North Sea. It is there that we now need to look to discover what effect depletion of British forces had on Berlin's decision to attack the East Coast.

Five

'German Spies Work From English Coast!'

With the announcement of war, many in the Royal Navy expected to be in full engagement with the enemy within two days – it was not to be. Indeed, the first true surface engagement in the North Sea was some time off. Minor skirmishes did occur, and as we have seen, submarine action brought about some spectacular early gains for the Imperial Navy, but as the year saw out, more concerted military efforts were planned and executed by both sides – culminating with the attack on the East Coast. Having discussed the events surrounding the outbreak of the war and subsequent action across the world's oceans, it is finally necessary to understand the situation in the North Sea and the East Coast of England. Only then can we place the attack on Scarborough, Whitby and Hartlepool into context.

Invasion

One real possibility was that the Germans might attempt an invasion of the British mainland, especially if the Royal Navy looked weak and there was an advantage to diverting the focus of the European campaign away from the Low Countries. This prospect began to look increasingly likely as the quick, decisive victory Germany had expected evaporated. The battles of Mons, the Marne, and Aisne saw the German advance become ever more sedentary until both sides began digging in. The hope that Calais could be taken and in so doing break the British hold over the Straits of Dover never materialised. So it was inevitable that, in desperation, the Reichstag began considering avenues intended to disrupt the flow of British troops and equipment into Northern France. Of course, this did not go unrecognised in London. Sir Arthur Wilson, First Sea Lord from 1910-11, argued that the current concentrations of the British fleet left much to be desired; the view that one major action should be sought with the enemy was both dated and dangerous. The key to lasting victory involved ensuring the enemy could not damage the Royal Navy in just such an action whilst always taking advantage of a good opportunity to damage the enemy. The answer was to disperse a large amount of the Royal Navy's strength, making it less vulnerable to attack. Dispersal also gave consistent protection down the coast, reducing the distances ships travelling at under 30 knots had to cover. Wilson noted,

> First, because there would be no possible chance of their arriving on the seen [*sic*] till many hours after the action was over; and secondly, because the object of the German main fleet in courting an engagement would probably be to enable a landing to be effected on the coast.

Wilson is probably most famous for stating that submarines were 'underhand, unfair and damned un-English'. His short time in office, followed quickly by Sir Francis Bridgeman and Prince Louis of Battenberg in the lead-up to war ensured most of Fisher's efforts to modernise the Royal Navy lost much of their drive.

The Committee of Imperial Defence had considered, since a speech delivered by Prime Minister Balfour on 11 May 1905, that, if an enemy launched an invasion of the United Kingdom, it would need to be more than 70,000 strong to reach London. Balfour also scuppered the notion supported during the Napoleonic War that the navy would keep any invaders from the British coastline; now co-operation between both services (army and navy) would be needed if a strong force was to be repelled. By early 1914, the topic of invasion had again raised its head. In a speech delivered at the Union Jack Club in London, the First Sea Lord, Prince Louis of Battenberg, warned against either service 'dispensing of the services of the other', again reiterating the inability of the Royal Navy to deal with a large invasion force alone. Clearly, an army of territorials were needed to defend the home shores; problem was since the Boer War, the credibility of such a force had been undermined by a lack of funding and training.

With the outbreak of war, preparations were made along the East Coast to repel enemy troops where necessary. Around Scarborough, observation posts, often in the form of trenches, were dug along the cliff tops. These were manned by territorials, local volunteers and, very occasionally, regular troops; to the north of the castle, this included men from Burniston Barracks. Territorial soldiers returned early from exercise in North Wales and deployed, with ammunition, around the town as early as the first week of August. As an extra precaution, the route up from the South Bay via Eastborough was sandbagged and all steps ascending from the foreshore were blocked with barbed wire and sandbags. Further north, it was a similar story.

Between Scarborough and Seaton Delaval, a territorial unit, the 7th (Cyclists) Battalion of the Devonshire Regiment, was deployed along the cliff top. Located close to villages and settlements so as to keep in contact by telephone, the men could do little other than observe the coastline and report any occurrences. Hartlepool, however, was a different story all together. At the outbreak of war, the defence of Hartlepool was almost exclusively undertaken by the Durham Royal Garrison Artillery (RGA), a territorial unit but one with far more potential 'clout' than its cyclist neighbours.

It is worth spending a few moments on the Durham RGA, as it has a connection with Scarborough, which, in turn, is important to the current work. At the turn of the century, the Royal Artillery was divided into the specific spheres, the Royal Field and Royal Horse Artillery and the Royal Garrison Artillery. As is so often the case

Above left: Routes up from the coast were very quickly barricaded on the declaration of war. Eastborough leading up from the foreshore in Scarborough was a good example of this.

Above right: The officers and men of the RGA and Durham RGA who were on station when the shells began to fall on Hartlepool.

in the military, the less glamorous but most scientific arm of the organisation, the coastal batteries, had traditionally received the under achievers from the officer corps. However, with restructuring and an all-important better rate of pay, the RGA became an effective force. Across the North East, three organisations, the Northumberland RGA, Durham RGA and East Riding of Yorkshire RGA manned the coastal batteries with a mixture of militia, regular and other voluntary irregulars. Crucially, until 1905, this force, known collectively as the North Eastern Group, had its depot and headquarters at Scarborough.

Post-Boer War, the land forces in the United Kingdom were in disarray. The Secretary of State for War, Richard Haldane, took the line that two distinct but similar forces were required if Britain were to maintain a credible defence of the Islands. By 1 April 1908, the Expeditionary and Territorial Forces had been formed. Within the Territorials was the provision for defending ports, including the manning and operation of coastal batteries and the erection of obstacles to deny the enemy easy passage inland from the coast. With regards to gunnery, the tide had been steadily turning away from fixed assets, as they were too vulnerable to bombardment and extremely costly to move; subsequently, old Victorian emplacements were constantly re-equipped and updated, often in piecemeal fashion. Also affecting this was the move to the bigger-calibre dreadnoughts and their ability to stand off the coast in a blockade and so be out of reach of any weapon – by this time, the 6-inch quick-firing gun. Instead, the protected port would be so done with surface and submarine vessels; this was the case at Hartlepool but not Whitby or Scarborough. However, costal defences were still the only method available to land forces, and so their constant 'modernisation' was only to be expected.

The complexity of coastal defence continued to develop along side advancements in technology, especially communications. The original network had been reliant on observation, runners and semaphore, by early 1914, the telephone had been introduced along with an effective command and control system, searchlight batteries and radio directional wireless stations like the one at Sandy Bed near Scarborough. The war radio stations operated by the Coast Guard, Scarborough Castle, Whitby and Hartlepool all had one by 1914, reported directly to the Admiralty. However, they were also in contact with local fire control officers if a coastal battery was present on that stretch of coastline.

Hartlepool had a coastal defence network that originated in the mid-nineteenth century. On 7 December 1859, the War Department leased land from Hartlepool Corporation for the purposes of building a battery, and late in 1860, the Heugh and Lighthouse Batteries were commissioned at a cost of £3,298; the original armament comprised four 68-pdr guns. In 1899, the Heugh Battery receive a major upgrade which culminated in two 6-inch breach-load guns being installed; this work practically swept away any evidence of the original defences. By 1914, the site benefitted from a depression rangefinder post, intended to triangulate and determine the azimuth of an object at sea level, and telephonic communications. Hartlepool, unlike Scarborough and Whitby, also enjoyed other defensive measures.

Floating Coastal Defence

Whilst discussion surrounding the part coastal defences played on 16 December 1914 is better left until later, it is, however, worth expanding on the naval defences at Hartlepool now. As part of the dispersal of naval power, the 3rd Division of the 9th Flotilla was stationed in Hartlepool docks. The force comprised two light (scout) cruisers, HMS *Patrol*, captained by the senior naval officer Alan C. Bruce, and HMS *Forward*. Attached to them were four river-class destroyers, HMS *Doon*, *Waveney*, *Test* and *Moy*. Also forming part of the division was the submarine C9 commissioned on 18 June 1908. The 9th Flotilla was an assortment of aged vessels, known in the Admiralty as the 'Floating Coastal Defence', dispersed up and down the East Coast. The principle base was at Dover under the command of Rear Admiral George Ballard; the position title was Admiral of Patrols. Ballard was something of a pioneer in naval tactics; he was required to plug the gap between the Channel and Grand Fleets with a collection of extremely light destroyers and submarines. To cover this vast stretch of coastline, he also utilised one of the newest technological innovations – aviation.

Two very different modes of aerial vehicle would become open to the Royal Navy as the war developed, but in the early stages, the use of aviation was sporadic to say the least. Interestingly, at Scarborough, the Blackburn Aeroplane & Motor Co. Ltd had built a shed at Scalby Mills, to the north of the town. It was intended to be a staging post for the *Daily Mail*-sponsored 'Circuit of Britain' race scheduled for 14 August 1914. Naturally, the outbreak of war ten days earlier put paid to any thoughts of the race, as all aircraft were immediately impounded by the War Office. The Blackburn Type L flew reconnaissance missions from Scalby Mills until its untimely demise when it flew into cliffs at Speeton, to the south of the town, in early 1915. There is no report of this early machine playing any part in the action undertaken on 16 December, but it seems unlikely that the aircraft left the relative safety of the flight shed.

Above left: HMS *Forward* formed part of the 3rd Division of the 9th Flotilla stationed at Hartlepool. The 9th Flotilla was known in the Admiralty as the 'Floating Coastal Defence'.

Above right: HMS *Patrol*, another component of the 3rd Division stationed at Hartlepool.

Blackburn Type L. Aviation was still in its infancy at the outbreak of war. This aircraft was stationed at Scalby Mills near Scarborough but took no part in the 'defence' of the East Coast.

By mid-November 1914, Ballard's forces had become dangerously dispersed. The original War Office order stipulated the flotillas should consider themselves the first line of defence against invasion. Unfortunately, the German Navy constantly sent out mine-laying missions and Ballard's ships, primarily the destroyers, had been deployed often singularly against them. Short on fuel, in need of repair or often forced to give up the chase due to bad weather, the destroyers would put into the nearest port. Now, if an invasion were launched, the flotillas were too dispersed along the coast to be of any great use. The threat of invasion was brought into sharp focus on 3 November, when German ships conducted the first raid on the British coastline.

On 2 November, Admiral Franz Ritter von Hipper, commanding a German squadron comprising SMS *Seydlitz*, *von der Tann*, *Moltke*, *Blucher*, *Strasburg*, *Graudenz*, *Kolberg* and *Stralsund* set out from the Jade River for a raid on the British coast. Franz Ritter von Hipper, born on 13 September 1863 in Weilheim, Oberbayern, joined the German Imperial Navy in 1881 at the age of eighteen. He was responsible for the development of the German torpedo boat force, commanding it until 1903. By October 1913, he had assumed command of the High Seas Fleet Scouting Force, comprising a number of battle cruisers. The intention was to lay mines, shell the coastal towns of Great Yarmouth and Gorleston and in so doing entice the Grand Fleet, or at least elements of it, to engage the German

SMS *Moltke* took part in the operation against Great Yarmouth on 3 November. A few weeks later she would be off the coast of Hartlepool, this time enjoying more success.

squadron. Hipper was to destroy as many ships as possible before leading the Royal Navy over mines and into a waiting curtain of dreadnoughts stationed just off the German coast. Early on the morning of 3 November, the squadron was discovered by the minesweeper HMS *Halcyon*, who immediately issued a challenge, she came quickly under fire but was rescued by a smoke screen from the supporting destroyers *Lively* and *Leopard*.

Whilst mines were being laid, the German squadron trained its guns on the coast, and just before eight o'clock in the morning, Britain felt the first shells by an enemy power close to her shores. Damage was negligible; indeed, all that happened was the beach was ploughed up at the low-water line, but even this was hotly disputed later in the press. That said, three submarines were dispatched from Great Yarmouth to intercept; unfortunately one, D5, struck a British mine protecting the harbour with the loss of twenty men. Initially, the Germans losses were nil; however, the dreadnought screen anchored off the German coast put paid to that. Fog-bound for a day, the captain of the SMS *Yorck* decided to sail for Wilhelmshaven without the proper clearance, became disorientated and ended up in the protective minefield. The ship struck two mines and went down, luckily in shallow water as many men were able to use the hull as an impromptu raft whilst waiting for rescue; that said, over 250 men were still lost. In terms of effectiveness, the raid was pretty much a disaster. Hipper was awarded the Iron Cross for the operation but refused to wear it, as he too thought it a less-than-successful venture. However, like all things in war, the implications were to rattle through the Admiralty and Whitehall and naturally all possible avenues were discussed through the newspapers.

YARMOUTH NOT BOMBARDED
London Newspapers Ridicule German Report of the Raid
Special Cable to *The New York Times*

London, Nov. 8. – There is no truth whatsoever in the German report that their ships bombarded Yarmouth. The German official reports speak of Yarmouth 'forts' but nothing of the kind exists. No shells from the German squadron fell on the land, although a few fell in the sea near the shore.

The English newspapers refer facetiously to the German claim as a good specimen of German mendacity. The *Daily News* says: 'All the German cruisers did was to attack the coastguard gunboat *Halcyon*, and then run away when our cruisers arrived.'

The New York Times
9 November 1914

Of course other areas of national concern were bound to appear: 'GERMAN SPIES WORK FROM ENGLISH COAST. Naval Information Signalled to 'Neutral' Fishermen, Who Pass It On by Carrier Pigeon,' claimed the Special Correspondent for *The New York Times* in London. And far from being viewed as hysterical, the matter made its way quickly through the House of Commons and onto the Lords.

Mr Joynson-Hicks (Conservative)
There is widespread anxiety with regard to spying on the East Coast. There is widespread anxiety with regard to the naval disasters we have had on the East Coast. There is a widespread feeling that signals have been given from the East Coast to the German Navy by which disasters have taken place. How about the loss of those three cruisers? There is a widespread belief that there were signals either by wireless or somehow that enabled the submarine to get in, and that there was also some means by which the mine chart off the East Coast was known to the German flotilla that came over to Yarmouth ten days ago.

Treatment of Alien Enemies
HC Deb 12 November 1914 vol. 68 cc79-123

And in the Lords a few days later:

I know nothing of this matter except what I see in the newspapers, but there was one item in the newspapers the other day which surely showed that information of enormous value had gone out of this country – I refer to the attempted raid on Yarmouth. We saw it stated that large enemy ships went at full speed through the passages of a mine field. A passage through a mine field is a crooked passage, and no enemy ship could possible go through a crooked passage without the most valuable information having left this country. It is possible, if that kind of information does go out of the country, that one item of information might lead in some case to a great national disaster.

Baron St Davids, John Phillips
HL Deb 18 November 1914 vol. 18 cc65-83

Not withstanding concerns surrounding spies and enemy agents across the English coast or fishing fleets, the action off Great Yarmouth forced a reorganisation of Admiral Ballard's forces. By mid-November, orders were given to restore the original division numbers across the East Coast, whilst the prevention and clearing of mines became the responsibility of the Auxiliary Patrols. The two large flotillas directly under Ballard's control were organised into four divisions; only one from each was to be in repair at any given time. The 7th Flotilla was massed at Great Yarmouth with two divisions and a further one on the Humber. The 9th held one division on the Tyne and on the Humber; the third patrolled between Flamborough Head and Hartlepool. It was this division that was in Hartlepool on the morning of 16 December.

The Auxiliary Patrols

To supplement the Royal Navy's coastal numbers, the government mobilised a large number of trawlers, merchant ships and drifters to assist in the blockading of ports and increasingly on submarine and mine spotting/trawling duties. The situation was eloquently summarised by Sir Julian Corbett in 1921:

> With sure instinct it was to the old well-spring of our sea power we went to renew our youth for the anxious contest. The fleet would no longer suffice, but behind it were still the deep-sea fishermen and the great seafaring population to whom nothing afloat came amiss.
>
> Over 150 trawlers and drifters had already been taken up, besides yachts and other small vessels, and as far as possible they were fitted with guns and explosive sweeps. As the men threw themselves into the work their increasing skill and enterprise proved the utility of the new force, and the cry for more became insatiable. Already during November the Commander-in-Chief had been promised for Scapa four units, each consisting of a yacht and twelve trawlers; Vice-Admiral Sir David Beatty at Cromarty was to have three yachts and eighteen trawlers, and these only for securing free movement for the Grand Fleet in the vicinity of its bases. Everywhere else, in the Straights of Dover, the English Channel, the Irish Sea, and especially in northern waters, the demand was scarcely less. In all tradition it had been a constant duty of the Grand Fleet to protect our fishing fleets; now it was the fishing fleets that must protect the Grand Fleet.
>
> Sir Julian S. Corbett
> Naval Operations Vol. II
> *History of the Great War based on Official Documents*, p. 2

The fact was submarines, and moreover the tactical advantage they provided, were quickly changing the face of naval warfare, as was the humble mine. Unlike the submarine, the mine was not a recent addition to naval warfare – early examples can be traced back as far as the Ming Dynasty, and the first British ship lost to an electrically discharged device was HMS *Merlin* in 1855 during the attempt on the port of Kronshtadt. During the Russo-Japanese conflict (1904-05), mines were used extensively causing major casualties on both sides; however, the British and German authorities elected to use the weapon in totally different ways. Mine warfare for the Royal Navy lacked much of the glamour associated with bringing enemy ships into action, so when war was declared, the British had practically no minesweeping capability. The German High Command, for their part, considered the mine an important part of their arsenal and a possible way of damaging and containing the Grand Fleet, an assumption strengthened on 27 October as one of the Royal Navy's newest dreadnoughts, HMS *Audacious*, struck a mine off the north coast of Ireland.

The ship stayed afloat for the rest of the day whilst attempts were made to tow her back to the protected anchorage at Lough Swilly; however, she eventually sank after a further explosion at 21.00. The loss of *Audacious* was a major blow to the Royal Navy's strength, so much so that the War Office refused to admit her sinking. A news blackout was imposed on the British press, although there was actually no way of maintaining this; the White Star Liner *Olympic* en route from New York had assisted in lifting off her crew and attempted to tow her to safety. Many on board took photographs of the event, and irrespective of the request for secrecy, the story appeared across the world. 'Wrecked in the North Sea; Big Superdreadnought Blown Up Off Irish Coast on Oct 27' front-paged *The New York Times* on 15 November, and it carried a full account from the *Olympic*'s crew the following day. Undeterred, Admiral John Jellicoe demanded the sinking be kept a secret, as *Audacious* counted for around 1/20th the super-dreadnought strength; the fact she was claimed by a mine would undoubtedly encourage the German Navy to sow even more of the cheap and evidently very effective devices.

Beyond coastal waters, the defence of the northern approaches, North Sea and Channel were a far more expensive and politically charged undertaking. By mid-November, an unlikely trio (Churchill, Fisher and Jellicoe) were making some important decisions about the distribution of the Grand Fleet and lesser flotillas. Each had a major hand in what was to develop but it was down to Admiral Sir John Jellicoe, the man who Churchill once noted was 'the only man on either side who could lose the war in an afternoon', to ensure the North Sea and beyond was denied to the enemy.

Jellicoe joined the Royal Navy as a cadet on 15 July 1872, seeing his first action ten years later during the Egyptian War. Promoted to Commander in 1891, he was executive officer on the iron-clad HMS *Victoria* when she was rammed by HMS *Camperdown* off the coast of Syria (now the Lebanon) in June 1893. By 1907, Jellicoe had influenced the development of fire-control systems within the new dreadnought class and the building of the submarine strength. At the outbreak of war, Jellicoe was installed as Admiral of the Grand Fleet, replacing the older George Callaghan, Commander of the British Home Fleet. This had always been planned in the event of war; however, Jellicoe still attempted to resist the appointment until ordered to take it up by Winston Churchill.

Jellicoe considered the navy's remit could be divided into four main tasks. The unimpeded use of the sea due to Britain's island status; deny the enemy use of the sea through constant presence; the protection of the army (British Expeditionary Force); to protect the Homeland or Dominions from invasion by an enemy force. In the case of Germany, this could be simply achieved. The majority of the High Seas Fleet's proposed operational area was in the North Sea; in fact, Germany had no options but to use the North Sea as she was land-locked in all other respects. Basing the Grand Fleet at Scapa Flow, a large open bay in the Orkneys, and the Channel Fleet on the South Coast would effectively deny the High Seas Fleet access to open water.

Above left: HMS *Audacious* flounders after she struck a mine. Here the majority of her crew take to the lifeboats. This shot was taken from the ocean liner *Olympic*.

Above right: The threat of spies was never far from everyone's thoughts. This poster from the United States in 1916 graphically demonstrates how the propaganda war advanced.

Above left: HMS *Liverpool* attempts to tow the stricken *Audacious* into port. It was to no avail; the super-dreadnought, estimated to be 1/20th of the Royal Navy's battleship capability, sank that evening.

Above right: Admiral Sir John Jellicoe. Churchill described him as 'the only man on either side who could lose the war in an afternoon'.

By early November, the majority of Jellicoe's fleet was stationed at the Orkneys, including twenty dreadnoughts and four battle cruisers; complementing this was the 6th and 10th Cruiser Squadrons carrying out northern water patrols. The Channel Fleet was also a major force comprising eighteen pre-dreadnought battleships and a multitude of other ships located around the South East Coast. Complementing the main fleet was the 'Harwich Force' boasting thirty-five destroyers and a number of light cruisers and connected to these large formations were the Auxiliary patrols. However, it was the big ships that were considered extremely vulnerable. Especially since the *Cressy*, *Hogue* and *Aboukir* had fallen victim to a single submarine and the *Audacious* had been lost to a mine.

Interestingly, the Kaiser played, unknowingly for the Royal Navy at the time, right into their hands, as he expressly forbade using the High Seas Fleet in any major action, ordering the use of mines and submarines wherever possible to wear down the enemy. This lack of foresight allowed the British to move vast quantities of men and equipment across the Channel and into Northern France unmolested. Meanwhile, the dispatch of battleships to the South Atlantic following the loss of Craddock at Coronel had made the prospect of an all-out confrontation an even more daunting possibility for Jellicoe. There had yet to be a major engagement in the North Sea and currently the High Seas Fleet patrolled the Baltic with near impunity. In London, the Admiralty thought this would not and could not last for much longer. The British blockade and disruption of the majority of shipping supply routes would soon be a major concern to the German Government and was bound to bring the fleet out of port. Whichever way one looked, it appeared clear the High Seas Fleet would make some sort of move soon. As we have already considered, a disruption in the flow of troops to France would, in all likelihood, have a major effect on the outcome of the Western Front. What the Germans needed was some way of persuading the British to commit large numbers of troops to home defence; key to that was to make London believe a major raid or even invasion was imminent. To defend against such an event required the co-ordination of not only the Floating Coastal Defence under Ballard's command, the coastal guns manned by the RGA or even the under-trained Territorials, it also required heavy back-up available in timely fashion. Any invading force was likely to come in numbers and be well organised; the fire power of the Grand Fleet would most definitely be needed if the Germans embarked on such a venture. The main problem was that the Grand Fleet, currently employed as a blockade force to the Baltic and northern access to the North Sea, was simply too far north to be effective. A reorganisation of forces would be needed at the battleship level to complete the protection of the East Coast.

Jellicoe also had concerns over his margin of superiority. The Grand Fleet was light a number of key assets, the *Audacious* needed to be replaced and the two vessels earmarked for this would take at least six to eight weeks to work up to full strength. It was also becoming increasingly clear that ships in Scapa Flow were very difficult to protect, especially against the ever-increasing effectiveness of enemy submarines. Scapa Flow, whilst large enough to contain many ships, had several routes of access. Not all were easy to control, and the destroyers that patrolled these areas had been depleted, as twelve were detached to the Channel on escort duties. By the second week of November, Jellicoe's worries were added to, as Churchill dispatched the *Inflexible* and *Invincible* to the South Atlantic to deal with von Spee. Then, on 11 November, HMS *Niger*, a torpedo gun boat, was sunk by submarine U-12 off the coast of Deal; the following day, Jellicoe was told to expect the return of the destroyers. Even then, the margin was far less than the ideal. At the start of the war, the Royal Navy held a 20:30 advantage; by the middle of November, this had reduced to 17:15 in the North

Sea. The introduction of Fisher's dreadnought had indeed allowed the Imperial Navy to reach parity, and it could still yet spell disaster.

Of course, there were other ways to counter the submarine threat. The range of such machines was limited, running on a diesel engine forcing it to stay on the surface made the vessels vulnerable. It wasn't long before the Imperial Navy were making use of captured Belgian ports to launch submarine missions into the North Sea, especially from facilities in Zeebrugge. When the area had been evacuated in the face of the advancing German Army, it was decided not to blow up any of the port facilities, this proved to be very unwise. As the possibility of retaking Zeebrugge became evermore distant, the Admiralty explored ways of rendering the port useless to enemy shipping. First on the list was blocking ships, sinking redundant vessels as obstacles; however, the work invested in doing this would put a sizable amount of Royal Navy ships within range of some impressive coastal guns, and the idea was abandoned in favour of bombardment. Shelling coastal ports and facilities was not the preserve of the German forces; quite a number of operations were undertaken by the British and French throughout the war. Those undertaken prior to the bombardment of the East Coast are worth recounting here, as they are important and go some way to explaining the High Seas Fleet's actions on 16 December.

A number of light attacks had taken place on Belgian ports from early October, but by mid-November, it had become clear major civil engineering works were underway at Zeebrugge. The likely reason was to build a submarine facility intended to threaten cross-channel communications. On 21 November, a force comprising two battleships, eight destroyers and a flotilla of minesweepers set off for the Belgian coast. Progress was slow, as most of the minesweepers were converted trawlers capable of 5-6 knots. On the morning of the 23rd, the force bombarded the port with over 400 shells. 'British Ships Smash Germans' Belgian Base' reported the *Daily Express*. However, reports from Rotterdam to *The New York Times* said otherwise:

ZEEBRUGGE LOSSES HEAVY
British Shells Destroyed a Big Hotel and Many Houses
Special Cable to *THE NEW YORK TIMES*

ROTTERDAM, Nov. 25. – Refugees who have arrived from the Belgian coast report the Zeebrugge suffered severely as the result of its bombardment by the British fleet on Monday. Much of the little town is in ruins.

The fleet appeared unexpectedly out of the mist, and the first gun fired dropped a shell in a group of military engineers engaged in work on a submarine in dry dock. Seventeen men were killed on the spot and a number wounded. The Palace Hotel, a fine building, erected last year, was levelled to the ground by the subsequent bombardment with high explosive shells, and two other hotels were also badly damaged. A large briquette factory was burned to the ground and sixteen private houses were practically destroyed.

The New York Times
26 November 1914

Not long after the event, the Admiralty learnt that the raid had actually done little damage; an electricity generating facility was destroyed but that had been it. Zeebrugge still posed a major threat to Channel shipping. Plans were discussed about revisiting the port on 14-15 December, but with naval intelligence suggesting something big was brewing in the major German ports, this was put on hold.

A Plan Comes Together

Throughout the early stages of the war, Tirpitz had wanted to use the High Seas Fleet offensively. He had planned specifically for an all-out, decisive blow against the Royal Navy and recognised the earlier this happened the more successful it was likely to be. Adhering to his Risk Theory, first suggested in 1900 as a component of the Second Navy Law, Tirpitz knew that the British would try to close down German open water operations as soon as was physically possible. Aiding this restriction was the launch of new ships, primarily through accelerated war production, coupled with advancements in anti-submarine and anti-mine warfare using airships and a huge minesweeper fleet quickly built up through auxiliary forces. Risk, the reader will remember, intended to strike at the heart of the Royal Navy whilst its forces were globally dispersed, and in so doing cause damage to an extent that another third country might seize the opportunity and also strike the British fleet. Unfortunately, by 1914, the only likely candidates were now allies of Britain, the rest had been overrun by the German advance or not yet recovered from previous wars. Subsequently, the Kaiser elected to keep the High Seas Fleet in reserve rather than commit to an all-out fight. Instead, a limited war or *Kleinkrieg* was adopted, and whilst this preserved the German fleet, it had a detrimental effect on the navy's morale. Men ready and trained for the fight had to sit back and accept the ridicule heaped on them from the army, indeed the whole question of navy funding was discussed in the Reichstag on more than one occasion in light of its apparent inability to fight.

Kleinkrieg did not, however, place a ban on the laying of mines or the bombardment of coastal sites. Mines had been laid in British coastal waters from pretty much the declaration of war. On 5 August, HMS *Amphion* and two destroyers had come upon the *Königin Luise*, a hastily pressed into service excursion vessel, laying mines off Harwich. The destroyer HMS *Lance* fired on the German ship and sunk her, the first shots of the naval conflict for Britain. Ironically, HMS *Amphion* struck one of the mines laid the previous day and became the first shipping loss of the Royal Navy. Since those early days, the North Sea had become the most difficult sea area in the world to navigate due to mines. The other, more relevant aspect of operations the Kaiser was happy to commit to was coastal bombardment; it was only a matter of time before the East Coast was brought into the equation. Admiral Gustav Heinrich Ernst Friedrich von Ingenohl, Commander of the High Seas Fleet, was in favour of an all-out attack but planned as directed for limited warfare. Attempting to wear the Royal Navy down and subsequently gain the numerical advantage, Ingenohl repeatedly chased for the fight. However, the first major action was on British terms on 28 August in what has become known as the First Battle of Heligoland Bight. Scouting missions by British submarines had recognised that, in true Teutonic fashion, a destroyer sweep was undertaken in the Bight at the same time every day. Here was an opportunity to deal a blow to the Germans and maybe entice out some light cruisers in the destroyers defence, subsequently attacking them with submarines. By the end of the day, the Imperial Navy had lost three light cruisers, had major damage inflicted on three more and lost a destroyer; the Royal Navy suffered only light damage. Naturally, the Kaiser was even more reluctant to let the High Seas Fleet take the fight to the enemy. Any operation now needed the royal seal of approval; Tirpitz protested loudly against the 'fundamental error of such a muzzling policy', but the Kaiser stuck to his decision and as Churchill later noted 'not a dog stirred from August till November'. The 'muzzle' now steadily strangled the life out of the German mariners, leaving Ingenohl with an even bigger morale problem. The only way out was to invoke some sort of action against the enemy – and quickly.

Initially, the resumption of merchant raiding was proposed in an attempt to lure out the Grand Fleet, German intelligence suggested the fear of submarines and mines was the reason the fleet remained in dock; it had not yet received news of the British detachment heading to the South Atlantic. Early indications were that coastal bombardment was a far more likely option if elements of the Grand Fleet were to be engaged. The action off Great Yarmouth, though very limited in success, had forced the Royal Navy to rethink its strategy; a basic plan outlining key objectives was submitted to the Kaiser on 16 November for approval. With Coronel fresh in his mind, the Kaiser approved the bombardment of Scarborough and Hartlepool along with the disabling of the coastguard wireless station at Whitby. Whilst the bombardment was underway, fresh mines were to be laid 6 miles off the point of attack in such a way as to impede any Royal Naval involvement whilst giving Ingenohl the opportunity to lure enemy shipping on to them if possible. The rearrangement of Ballard's squadrons into coastal patrols with two squadrons stationed on the Humber and the concentration at Harwich were also identified as likely targets. It was almost certain that these vessels would be dispatched to counter the attack, and when they emerged from port, German submarines would be waiting for them. The main operation was to run from 22-24 November with some submarine work to run a further two days. By the 19th, the initial plan had been given the go-ahead.

The details of such a daring raid were comprehensive. First and foremost, there was the problem of navigating the suspected minefields along the East Coast. Since the onset of the war, mines had been sown along the coast; some by the British as protection against raiders but most by the Germans as traps for merchantmen or the coastal protection vessels. The problem was there was no real way of knowing how much of the offensive minefields survived, how much the minesweepers had removed and more importantly how much the British had added to them. Intelligence taken from Dutch and Danish captains working the East Coast suggested that the minefields were marked, but not very clearly. There were routes in from open water, and the Royal Navy had told any vessel following the shore to 'hold close under the coast', suggesting that nothing dangerous lurked in shallow water.

The only way to have more reliable intelligence was to physically investigate. So, on 21 November, submarine U-27 was dispatched on a reconnaissance mission to map the minefields. U-27 was a new boat, commissioned on 8 May 1914; her crew captained by Kapitänleutnant Bernd Wegener, were already expert at monitoring enemy shipping and positions off the coast of Flanders and France. Keeping his crew in the dark for fear of the mission leaking out, Wegener sailed to Whitby on 21 November before running up and down the coast between Scarborough and Hartlepool. On the 26th, he was able to report that numerous vessels were using the routes under the coast and the suspected minefield on the approaches was not as dense as was first thought. The westerly route into Whitby appeared especially clear, and Wegener suggested in his report that this would be the most effective route into the targets.

The problem with press reporting in the early twentieth century, especially through neutral countries' newspapers, was that the editor often included anything that he considered would increase circulation. And nothing increased circulation more than naval action; with one short article, it looked like the element of surprise had been lost.

SAY GERMAN FLEET PREPARES FOR ACTION
Fishermen Report Plans for Decisive Campaign in the North Sea

LONDON, Nov. 22. – Messages from North Holland say that unusual activity prevails at Emden, says a dispatch from the Exchange Telegraph Company's correspondent at The Hague. The telegram continues:

  'Fishermen who daily cruise near the German waters say that the German Fleet is preparing for decisive action in the North Sea. Prince Henry of Prussia was at Emden yesterday for an inspection of the torpedo and submarine craft.'

The New York Times
23 November 1914

Luckily, the weather delayed any possibility of traversing the North Sea without accruing damage to the fleet, and so the story slipped into obscurity. Indeed, the weather was so bad U-27 had to wait until 8 December before she could undertake a further sweep of the operational area. That said, the German High Command were only too aware that if they were sending out reconnaissance missions, the British, if they had taken notice of the newspaper reports, might well be doing the same. What the British were actually doing was following the build-up by monitoring the German wireless signals through a newly created organisation – the Intelligence Division or Room 40 as it was better known. The First World War ushered in new ways of conducting warfare, and radio intelligence gathering was yet another direct result of the march of technology. Advances in radio, especially wireless communication at sea, became the key to many naval operations; however, it was fairly indiscreet when it came to who could listen in. So as the medium developed so did ways of encrypting messages through complex codes. Room 40 was set up in the old Admiralty building to explore the opportunities a series of fortuitous discoveries posed. On 26 August, the light cruiser SMS *Magdeburg* ran aground off the Estonian coast. Before the crew had time to destroy the code books, the Russian Navy had arrived, and by mid-October, the books were with the Admiralty. A further set of books was found on board a German steamer near Australia, and on 30 November, a lead chest was trawled up that contained further vital shipping codes. All these discoveries allowed the British to successfully intercept and decode German radio traffic.

Room 40 was now predicting a raid on the coast; however, the organisation was still not mature enough to give precise details. For their part, the German forces protected themselves against prying eyes by running a sweep off Heligoland on 10 December. Included in the operation was SMS *Kolberg*; she would be off Scarborough a few days later. The operation had also taken on a new sense of urgency as, by now, the first reports were coming in of a major catastrophe for the Imperial Navy. On the same day U-27 returned to the North Sea, the Reichstag learnt of the destruction of von Spee and his squadron in the South Atlantic. Not withstanding the need for a morale boost, Ingenohl also realised that at least three British battle cruisers must not be with the Grand Fleet. Now, at this moment of weakness, was the time to strike.

On 11 December, two submarines, U-28 and U-32, set sail for the Humber, their primary objective, watching for Ballard's divisions from the 7th and 9th Flotillas stationed on the river. U-32 never made it; the weather closed in again and she had engine trouble due to the ingress of water. By the 13th, she had been replaced by U-30; Wegener in U-27 was not fairing much better. The storm had reached such epic proportions that she had to submerge to escape it, but not before the radio aerial had been damaged, meaning there was little chance of transmitting in any information. It was not until the 14th that Wegener was able to report that the lanes still appeared clear of obstacles. The following day, Kontreadmiral Hipper received his orders. The operation was to begin the following night, and at 03.00 hrs on 15 December, Ingenohl and Hipper's units left the River Jade and headed north. Later, Admiral Scheer, Ingenohl's successor, recorded,

> On December 15 the big cruisers under the command of Vice-Admiral Hipper sailed under orders to bombard the fortified coast towns of Scarborough and Hartlepool and to lay mines along the coast, for there was constant traffic between the East Coast ports. Both these places, however, are 150 nautical miles nearer to the chief bases of the English Fleet in the North of the British Isles than is Yarmouth. It would, therefore, be much easier for vessels lying there or cruising at sea in the vicinity to beat off an attack, and the expedition would probably present a much greater risk, and a more urgent call for support from the Fleet.
>
> Germany's High Seas Fleet in the War 1919

Although the Kaiser had expressly forbade any action involving the High Seas Fleet, it seemed unwise to allow a sizable attacking force to engage the enemy in such restricted close quarters without some form of back-up. As a pre-deployment measure, SMS *Moltke* was dispatched into the North Sea to monitor radio traffic. By 21.00, it appeared that the preparations for the movement of the 1st and 2nd Scouting

Above left: Submarine U-28 was scheduled to sit off the mouth of the Humber, waiting for Ballard's divisions.

Above right: Admiral Hipper. Hipper commanded the bombardment phase of the East Coast raid.

HMS *Shark*. One of Beatty's destroyers. The *Shark* shelled SMS *Hamburg* at just after 05.00 on the morning of 16 December.

Divisions comprising four battle cruisers, one heavy cruiser, four light cruiser and two destroyer flotillas; screened by a further nine cruisers and five destroyer flotillas had gone unnoticed. The 1st, 2nd and 3rd Battle Squadrons of the High Seas Fleet stood ready to intervene to the east of Dogger Bank by midnight whilst *Moltke* continued to monitor the airwaves, but very little came from the British.

Interestingly, the Royal Navy, although quiet, were not sleeping – far from it. Room 40, although not mature enough to give precise dates to information, had been following a major build-up of the Imperial Navy's fleet. By 14 December, they were in a position to give a warning of action being imminent – the Grand Fleet readied itself. The two flotillas stationed at Harwich were to shadow any enemy concentrations once discovered. The Grand Fleet would concentrate in northern areas. Admiral Beatty would take out four battle cruisers and attached aspects of the 4th Flotilla from Cromarty; Ballard's Floating Coastal Defence was also readied. Jellicoe sailed with the 2nd Battle Squadron comprising six dreadnoughts and one light cruiser. He was

Above left: Admiral Hipper's 1st Scouting Division comprised the following six ships: SMS *Derfflinger.*

Above right: SMS *von der Tann.*

Above: SMS *Blücher.*

Right: SMS *Moltke.*

to be met at sea by Commodore Goodenough, commanding the 1st Cruiser Squadron, a further five ships. Admiral Pakenham with the 3rd Cruiser Squadron joined on the afternoon of 15 December, and by early morning of the 16th, Commodore Tyrwhitt had arrived at the rendezvous point with the 5th Battle Squadron. Considering where the enemy might strike, the rendezvous point was set at 110 miles off Flamborough Head. The reasoning behind this was simple. From the outset of the war, mines by both sides had been liberally sown across the North Sea. Three large fields now narrowed the approaches to the English Coast, and considering an attack on a major naval installation was unlikely, there could be only one route to take – through the twenty-five-mile gap that faced Scarborough and Whitby. Jellicoe's decision to station where he did unknowingly placed him just 50 miles south-east of Ingenohl's re-muster point.

At just after 05.00 on the morning of 16 December, Beatty's destroyers encountered the enemy. Opening fire, both sides received damage. HMS *Hardy* managed to get a torpedo away, which unfortunately detonated too far from the enemy ship,

Above left: SMS *Seydlitz.*

Above right: SMS *Kolberg.*

SMS *Hamburg*, one of the advance light cruisers in Ingenohl's fleet. On learning this, Jellicoe was convinced he would see action. The *Hamburg* broke off far too early, suggesting it was not concerned about a few destroyers. Clearly something very big was following behind. At this point, the weather played its hand. The wind built up, forcing a high sea swell, so much so that Ingenohl called off the light cruisers and destroyers, sending them to the position of the Battle Squadron. Admiral Hipper was to continue on with the 1st Scouting Division and one light cruiser. This removal of Hipper's protection was a gamble. If the element of surprise was lost, it could have serious consequences. Indeed, Sir Julian Corbett suggested a few years later that the real reason Ingenohl sent the majority of ships to the rear was on account of the distance they now were from the German ports, 'knowing nothing of the presence of our squadrons, he fairly turned tail and made for home, leaving his raiding force in the air.' Just after 07.30, Hipper exited the coastal end of the minefield and his forces split into two. *Derfflinger* and *von der Tann* with *Kolberg* turned south, objective Scarborough, whilst *Seydlitz*, *Moltke* and *Blücher* headed north for Hartlepool.

Six

"Business as usual' is all very well, but there are limits!'

By 09.30, it was over, 135 lay dead across the three towns and more than 500 were seriously injured. Hartlepool's losses were by far the greater; however, it was the destruction in Scarborough that stirred the public's anger, ably stoked by the press and, in the background, the government. Two things drove this: the apparent lack of defence in and around Scarborough, and the probability that the town was far more familiar to the nation than Hartlepool. The town's population was applauded by the nation for keeping calm and maintaining a typical 'business as usual' attitude; however, it took a number of days to clear the debris and free people still trapped in the remnants of their homes. Letters of support began arriving at the Town Hall and newspaper offices within hours of the attack, a few of which are articulated below.

A statement from the Admiralty was issued the same day:

This morning a German cruiser force made a demonstration upon the Yorkshire coast, in the course of which they shelled Hartlepool, Whitby, and Scarborough. A number of their fastest ships were employed for this purpose, and they remained about an hour on the coast. They were engaged by the patrol vessels on the spot.

As soon as the presence of the enemy was reported, a British patrolling squadron endeavoured to cut them off. On being sighted by the British vessels the Germans retired at full speed, and, favoured by the mist, succeeded in making good their escape. The loss on both sides was small, but full reports have not yet been received.

Admiralty, 16 December 1914

The War Office followed up later that evening, noting,

At 8 a.m. to-day three enemy ships were sighted off Hartlepool, and at 8:15 they commenced a bombardment. The ships appeared to be two battle cruisers and one armoured cruiser. The land batteries replied, and are reported to have hit and damaged the enemy. At 8.50 the firing ceased. None of our guns were touched.

One shell fell in the R.E. lines, and several in the lines of the 18th Service Battalion of the Durham L.I. The casualties amongst the troops amounted to 7 killed and 14

Children in Hartlepool look
at some of the trophies on
display.

wounded. Some damage was done to the town, and the gasworks were set on fire.
During the bombardment, especially in Hartlepool, the people crowded the streets,
and approximately 22 were killed and 50 wounded.

At the same time a battle cruiser and an armoured cruiser appeared off Scarborough
and fired about 50 shots, which caused considerable damage, and 13 casualties are
reported. At Whitby two battle cruisers fired some shots, doing damage to buildings,
and the following casualties are reported, namely, two killed and two wounded. At all
these places there was an entire absence of panic, and the demeanour of the people
was everything that could be desired.

Berlin's response was initially limited; she still had ships at sea and didn't want to
jeopardise their safety. An official telegram intercepted in Amsterdam noted only that
'parts of the German High Seas Fleet made an attack on the English East Coast, and
bombarded early yesterday morning both the fortified coast places of Scarborough
and Hartlepool'.

Later, on 17 December, a further statement was issued:

When approaching the English coast our cruisers were unsuccessfully attacked by
four British destroyers in misty weather. One destroyer was sunk and the others
disappeared in a badly damaged condition. The batteries at Hartlepool were silenced
and the gasworks destroyed. Several detonations were heard and three big fires in the
town could be observed from our ships. The coastguard stations and waterworks at
Scarborough, and the signal station at Whitby were destroyed.

The German press were far less reserved, taking instead a triumphalism tone. 'A New
Courageous Deed by our Naval Forces. Bombarding of English Resorts: Panic in
Scarborough, Hartlepool and Whitby,' declared *The Nűrnburger Zeitung. The Berliner
Tageblatt* described the towns as 'fortified places' whilst in the *Neusten Nachrichten*
saw the attack as 'further proof of the gallantry of our Navy'.

Conflicting reports were inevitable at this early stage, a point clearly demonstrated
by the War Office release and the official German telegram. The story was further
confused, as traumatic events usually are, by eyewitness accounts taken out of context.

Damage in Gladstone Road. The school in this road was also damaged, thankfully too early to be full of children. The majority of damage across the town looked like this.

An account of the morning's attack appeared in *The Daily News* in London that evening citing '100 Houses in Flames'. The account was the experiences of Arthur Wood and his family, who had arrived at King's Cross Station from York. Mr Wood, head book-keeper with the Scarborough Electric Supply Co. suffered minor head injuries, primarily from flying glass, as did his twelve-year-old son Clifford, and after receiving treatment at the hospital, he had decided to move to the capital. Reporters usually stalked the railway stations of London looking for the famous or unusual and, having been tipped off that trains from the east could carry victims of the bombardment, were conspicuously evident on the platforms at King's Cross. Naturally, two people, 'each had his head swathed in bandages', alighting from a train tipped to be full of injured civilians was a tempting story source – the Woods were only too happy to oblige. The following quotation further demonstrates the fog of war.

> Shortly after the bombardment commenced a reply was made by the guns at the Castle. The east end of the town came in for more attention at the hands of the enemy than any other part of the town. When the firing had ceased there were, I should think, quite a hundred houses in this part of the town in flames.
>
> Arthur Wood as reported in *The Daily News*, 17 December 1917

'Fortress' Scarborough

It is worth pausing here to consider the comments made by Wood and the medium by which they were reported. *The Daily News* was founded by Charles Dickens in 1846, during the rapid expansion of the popular press in Victorian Britain. From 1901, it had been owned by George Cadbury, Quaker, well-known pacifist and no friend of central government. He had used the papers columns to make vehement comment on the Boer War, the lack of pensions for the working majority and the rights of 'sweated labour', mostly women home workers. Since August 1914, Cadbury had been openly criticising the government's involvement in the war in Northern Europe; the bombardment of the East Coast towns was clearly another example of how flawed Britain's European and foreign policy actually was. It should, therefore, come as no surprise that *The Daily*

A collage of the armament Scarborough had in her possession at the time of the bombardment. Published by the *Scarborough Mercury* a few weeks later.

News might report events in the extreme. Considering actual events, very little fire damage was reported across Scarborough, all the more remarkable when you consider the primary lighting for most homes was still town gas.

The reply by the castle guns was disputed by the Mayor of Scarborough the following day. The *Chicago Daily News* London Correspondent, Edward Price Bell, cabled a report of the bombardment from London to his head office, he quoted the Mayor C. C. Graham as saying,

> I want to correct the statement that guns on Castle Hill replied to the German fire. There is not a gun on Castle Hill and has not been for many years. At one time we had there a few old muzzle-loading forty and sixty pounders, but they have long since disappeared.

This is important and offers at least one avenue of investigation. A large network of coastal gun batteries had been built up during the Napoleonic Wars, nearly 150 artillery pieces were located on the North East Coast between Bamborough Castle and Hull alone. As the campaigns rolled across Europe, it became increasingly evident that the French were increasingly incapable of invasion; the batteries were steadily decommissioned. After Napoleon's disastrous invasion of Russia in 1812 and subsequent defeat in 1815 at Waterloo, the remaining batteries were disbanded and their guns withdrawn to armoury depots at Tynemouth, Berwick and, crucially, Scarborough.

In *Krieg zur See 1914-1918, Nordsee Band 3*, the Kriegmarine's official history, Scarborough was 'known' to have a battery of six 6-inch quick-firing guns and a further three unmounted. It was true that 6-inch guns were in evidence along the North East Coast. The manufacturer Vickers modified their successful design in 1898, introducing a pivot-mounted breach-loader capable of penetrating over 22 inches of iron with eight rounds per minute over 12,000 yards. From 1901, the weapon was in evidence at most coastal batteries, and in a demonstration of its effectiveness, some were still in use when the organisation was disbanded in 1956. Crucially, the Scarborough area did not contain a battery, indeed the closest travelling north was the South Gare Battery opened in 1892 on the mouth of the River Tees. To the south, work had only just started on the Humber defences at the outbreak of war.

However, on a postcard taken from one of the crew of the *von der Tann* when the ship was interred at Scapa Flow, Scarborough was depicted as returning fire on the German ships. It would be foolish to place too much importance on this one image, especially since it is an illustrated postcard for public consumption, but it could quite easily add to the perpetuation of Scarborough being a defended town.

Admiral Reinhard Scheer later wrote in his memoirs, *Germany's High Seas Fleet in the World War*, published in 1920,

> As there was no counteraction it must be assumed that the battery at Scarborough was either not manned in proper time, or had been evacuated by the garrison.

Clearly then, the German High Command considered Scarborough a defended town even though the possibility of a coastal battery threatening any seaborne invader had, in reality, long since gone. Now, one could argue that the Germans knew Scarborough was undefended, but protested their innocence in the face of mounting criticism; I think not. The point is we cannot entirely rule out the fact that Ingenohl may have considered his information on the status of Scarborough accurate; indeed, we could argue it was only a year old. In August 1913, the luxury cruise liner *Kronprinzessin Cecilie* anchored just off Scarborough; it was in the process of returning around 250 German medical staff who had attended a conference in London. The visitors were afforded all the usual pleasantries by the town; many were officially received at a reception held at the Town Hall prior to a guided tour of the castle and its surrounding buildings. It is highly likely that at the time of the visit to Scarborough some guns were still in storage or it was mentioned to

Kronprinzessin Cecilie visited Scarborough in August 1913. Many on board were given a VIP tour of the town, including the castle. At the start of the war, she was interned by the USA and is shown here at Bar Harbor. (C. McCutcheon)

the group that the eighteenth-century barracks had been used for such a purpose. That coupled with a discussion about the south-steel battery, at one time described as the finest coastal battery in England, could quite easily have been mistranslated. It is not beyond the realms of possibility that the recollections, diaries and reports from this visit were later passed to the Imperial Navy. Inevitably, the talk turned to spies as the following extract published on 19 December 1914 in *The New York Times* demonstrates:

> The authorities, especially those concerned with coastal defence, are investigating some strange coincidences in connection with the German raid. All the facts point to intimate knowledge of the localities on the part of the commanders of the German warships.

Taking into account the bombardment of the castle, this was a fair assumption; however, its validity was quickly lost on reading further:

> It may be said that it is easy to gain exact acquaintance with the position of a railway station, for instance, by the use of an ordnance map or the ordinary plan of a town, but the German gunners went further than that. They directed their fire at houses, hotels and other buildings where until recently men of the Yorkshire dragoons, yeomanry, and territorials were quartered for training purposes.

Obviously, this pinpoint accuracy is not in evidence, bar the destruction of the old barracks at the castle, but the extracts do serve to demonstrate the level of hysteria the press often promotes when news agencies are looking for a new angle. That said, there was growing resentment against foreign nationals across the United Kingdom. Scarborough, by the very nature of its business, contained hundreds of itinerant workers, mostly employed in the hotels, a large proportion of whom were Austrian or German. Naturally, they now came under the spotlight:

> Waiters Marched Out
>
> In fact it is said that at one hotel the head waiter drew up his staff and marched them out the day war was declared. The locality is one with which the Germans are intimately acquainted, and the fact that their wireless now announces the destruction of the water works is significant.
>
> *The New York Times*, 19 December 1914

The hysteria was not limited to the newspapers. The question of what should be done with 'Aliens' rapidly took centre stage after the Christmas recess, as this debate in the House of Lords illustrates:

> Lord Moncreiff
> After the raid on the East Coast, very curiously, forty aliens were within the next day expelled from Hartlepool. It seems to me that it took a very long time to find out that they were not desirable people to have there.

Lord Nunburnholme

My Lords, I should like to ask the noble Marquess who leads the House to put into force stronger orders under the Defence of the Realm Act. Exactly twenty-four hours before the bombardment of Scarborough a German lady whom the police had placed under observation left the town. That looks rather curious, and as if she knew all about it. I might add that she has never been seen since. There are on the East Coast of Yorkshire in the prohibited areas a good many naturalised Englishmen and aliens, and many of the people in my county, in the towns on the coast, think that the time has come to clear out all these people en masse. We do not see why we should take any risks considering the state of war we are in. Many of these aliens and naturalised Englishmen may have resided in this country for many years and may be perfectly respectable people, but the general view is that no risks should be taken and that they should be either deported or interned.

The Earl Of Crawford

A great many aliens who are here will not go back. The noble Marquess himself knows the great, powerful, alien enemy influence there is in this country, and even at the expense of Government funds those men will not go back. It is the ordinary German or Austrian citizens who, if guaranteed a through passage home, would many of them go. If you repatriated the whole of the aliens at large in this country, it would not cost more than one and a half hours of the present cost of the war.

HL Deb 06 January 1915 vol. 18 cc272-86

Along with the possibility of out-of-date intelligence and the fear of a spy round every corner comes a record first started nearly 100 years previously. The War Office, in its eagerness to build an accurate picture of the United Kingdom's coastline during the Napoleonic period, surveyed all defensive coastal sites around the British Isles. In the immediate aftermath of the bombardment, it appeared this had come back to haunt the government:

It was brought to Sir E. Grey's notice that, according to the official nomenclature employed at the War Office, the term 'fortress' is applied to any place having permanent defences, irrespective of their military value, importance or size.

Secretary of the Army Council from the Foreign Office
31 December 1914
PRO WO/374/60612

The danger of misrepresentation is obviously clear and had been so for some time before the attacks on the East Coast. Between 4 December 1908 and 26 February 1909, the 'London Naval Conference' held session discussing a wide range of topics. Top of the British delegations agenda was the intent to form an International Prize Court. An official body to oversee claims of 'prize' – the acquisition of equipment, goods or vessels during war – primarily as an attempt to give international validity to the Royal Navy stopping German ships supplying the Boers at the turn of the century.

Eventually a broad document was produced containing 71 articles of maritime law, among them, article 33 and 34, which stated,

> Art. 33. Conditional contraband is liable to capture if it is shown to be destined for the use of the armed forces or of a government department of the enemy State, unless in this latter case the circumstances show that the goods cannot in fact be used for the purposes of the war in progress. This latter exception does not apply to a consignment coming under Article 24 (4).

> Art. 34. The destination referred to in Article 33 is presumed to exist if the goods are consigned to enemy authorities, or to a contractor established in the enemy country who, as a matter of common knowledge, supplies articles of this kind to the enemy. A similar presumption arises if the goods are consigned to a fortified place belonging to the enemy, or other place serving as a base for the armed forces of the enemy. No such presumption, however, arises in the case of a merchant vessel bound for one of these places if it is sought to prove that she herself is contraband.

Interestingly, not all governments had ratified the 'Declaration' by the outbreak of war. Just a short time before August 1914, British and German officials had discussed the interpretation of the phrases 'fortified place' and 'base for the armed forces of the enemy'. However, no formal agreement was reached, indeed,

> No formal instrument incorporating the agreement so arrived at was, it is true, actually signed, but the formula which the German Government signified their readiness to accept was embodied in a draft protocol.
>
> Foreign Office letter dated 29 December 1914
> PRO WO/374/60612

Again, one can infer a certain level of misinterpretation of the terminology here, especially when considering the definition of fortress and its German equivalent 'Festung', a generic term for a heavily fortified or defended place. In a clear reference to the events two weeks earlier, the Secretary for the Army Council made the following observation:

> Not only must the risk to neutrals of trading with British ports be greatly increased thereby, but the destruction of British lives and property may even result, since the German Government will be able to appeal to the fact that virtually undefended ports are officially described by His Majesty's Government as 'Fortresses' in justification of the bombardment of such places.
>
> Secretary of the Army Council from the Foreign Office
> 31 December 1914
> PRO WO/374/60612

From the outset of hostilities, the danger was clear. Shipping in British ports, whether it be a foreign neutral or not, would be considered a viable target by the German Navy;

all attempts would be aimed at making neutral countries think twice before trading with the 'enemy'. Furthermore, article 34 of the *Declaration of London* (1909) made the case for shelling any shipping that used a 'fortified place'; practically all British ports had some form of remnant defences and subsequently could, in international law, be attacked. The speed at which the government changed the terminology surrounding ports after the bombardment adds considerable weight to this argument that the Imperial Navy thought Scarborough was defended. The Secretary of State for War reassessed the situation and instructed some changes. The following letter from the Chief of the Imperial General Staff, Lieutenant-General Sir James Murray, succinctly demonstrates.

> The S of S has decided that as regards Coast Defences in the United Kingdom, the terms 'Garrison' and 'Garrison Commander' will in future be used instead of 'Fortress' (or Defended Port)' and 'Fortress' (or Defended Port) Commander'.
>
> The change in name will involve no alteration in the responsibility of the officers concerned, nor in the areas under their command.
>
> It is not proposed to correct existing official publications, but in all future orders, official communications, or correspondence, the terms 'Fortress' (or Defended Port)' and 'Fortress' (or Defended Port) Commander' will not be employed. The Commands are being notified accordingly.
>
> 13 January 1915
GIGS
PRO WO/374/60612

So, from then on, any town fitting the description offered in the *Declaration of London* would be know as a garrison and not a defended port or fortress, and then only if it did indeed have a credible defence. Unfortunately, the damage had, quite literally, been done by then. However, it was abundantly clear that Ingenohl had issued orders to destroy not only key sites involving manufacture, but specific military ones as well. At Hartlepool, the bombardment took account of the coastal batteries from the outset, stationing SMS *Blücher* in a position to keep the onshore guns occupied, whilst *Seydlitz* and *Moltke* took out industrial targets. At Whitby, the target was the East Cliff Signal Station near the Abbey, it was only when a smaller facility in the harbour was targeted that the majority of the damage was inflicted on the town. Indeed, we can say the only reason Whitby was attacked was the signal station and other wireless facilities. So, were there any similar 'legitimate' military targets at Scarborough?

Wireless

The answer to this question can be demonstrated by actions around the world. The *Emden*, you will recall, was in the act of destroying a wireless station on Direction Island when HMAS *Sydney* caught her. And, in the South Atlantic, von Spee intended to destroy the wireless station built on Wolf Rocks close to the Falkland Islands. The point is wireless stations were vital to both sides. However, those were not isolated incidents, nor were they the preserve of German forces. Just four days after Britain declared war, a Royal Navy light cruiser, HMS *Astraea* shelled Dar-es-Salaam, destroying the wireless station. On 12 August 1914, the armoured cruiser HMS *Minotaur* and light cruiser HMS *Newcastle* bombarded the wireless station on the Western Caroline Islands in the Pacific. Both Britain and Germany ran a vast network of stations around the globe, the only difference being the Royal Navy made use of an extensive cable network. In the Cameroons, British amphibious operations took the German wireless station in late September 1914, and the very first operation the Australian Navy undertook was the disabling of the station at Bita Paka in New Guinea by men landed by HMAS *Melbourne*. The Australians destroyed two further German stations in the Palau Islands and at Kabakaul in September, suffering their first casualties when the German native troops put up strong resistance.

Scarborough had, like Whitby, a war signal station, this time located on castle hill; it was destroyed in short order by the bombardment. However, one further facility also fits the bill: a wireless station situated two miles inland. The station at Sandy Bed had been built the year before the war, initially to pass messages out to the North Sea; however, it was also part of a new system of directional range finding. It is easy to forget that radio was still in its infancy when war broke out; it had quickly demonstrated itself to be invaluable to the navy, but direction application was developed by the army. Surprisingly, individual signallers became recognisable by the key-stroke style they had. If more than one station picked up the message, then the origin could be located through triangulation. If the operator moved to a different location, then it was a fair bet that his unit or battalion had moved. Naturally, this had even greater applications for the navy. Indeed, reflecting later on the war, Admiral Sheer had this to say about the capability employed during the East Coast raids:

> The English received the news through their 'directional stations' which they already had in use, but which were only introduced by us at a much later period. They are wireless stations for taking the directional bearings of wireless messages, and in combination are capable of indicating the direction from which intercepted wireless messages come and thus locating the signalling ship's station. The stretch of the English east coast is very favourable for the erection of these 'directional station'. In possessing them the English had a very great advantage in the conduct of the war, as they were able thus to obtain quite accurate information as to the locality of the enemy as soon as any wireless signals were sent by him. In the case of a large fleet, where separate units are stationed far apart and communication between them is essential, an absolute cessation of all wireless intercourse would be fatal to any enterprise.

The onus put on knocking out wireless stations around the world at the onset of war is therefore self-evident. Even though the Germans were yet to develop the directional aspects of the equipment they already found it indispensible in naval operations. To quote the *Scarborough Evening News*,

HOLE MADE BY A SHELL.

FALSGRAVE FARM.

Photos by Miss Roberts

These few shells were the closest the Germans got to the wireless station. Incidentally, GCHQ Scarborough is still operational – the oldest serving station in the United Kingdom. The station is now on the hill behind the couple in the left-hand picture.

Apparently the wireless station was an objective, as properties in the line of fire suffered, particularly at Falsgrave, but the wireless station itself remains intact.

17 December 1914

At the Wireless

The enemy evidently intended to destroy the wireless station. Large numbers of shells were directed at the station, but with one exception, the shells fell short. The soldiers on guard at once retired to a place of safety, some 100 yards to the rear of the wireless. Several workmen who were engaged in that vicinity had narrow escapes. One shell dropped only a few yards from the Red House, which is the residence at the top of Falsgrave Park, and one of the nearest to the Government's property. The shell shattered all the windows in the place. The shells mowed up tons of earth as they exploded on the hill in front of the wireless. One of the shells fell some ten yards from the receiving House, but no damage was done.

17 December 1914

Burniston Barracks

One other military site in the immediate area was Scarborough (known locally as Burniston) Barracks. Constructed in 1861-62, the brick-built barracks were intended as an Artillery Militia Depot for the East and North Yorkshire Corps founded in 1860. The militia comprised volunteers and ex-soldiers who gave four weeks service per year, permanent instructors were members of the Royal Artillery. By the turn of the century, the militias had been reorganised and the North Eastern Group had both headquarters and depot at Burniston; however, by 1906, a major reduction of armament saw the group disbanded and the barracks stood empty.

Mr Walter Rea

I beg to ask the Secretary of State for War whether the Burniston Road barracks at Scarborough which, since the removal of the Royal Garrison Artillery Depot, have almost ceased to be occupied, are well above the average in suitability, owing not only to their modern construction and healthy situation but to the considerable amount of land adjoining which has been purchased and placed at their disposal by the Corporation of Scarborough; and whether, having regard to those facts and in view of the loss to the State involved in keeping the buildings empty, he will endeavour to devise a plan by which they may be utilised for some special or other purpose which will entail their regular occupation.

Mr Haldane
Under present arrangements it has not been found practicable so far to quarter in Scarborough barracks more than a very small body of men. I am well aware of the advantages of the barracks, and I can assure my hon. friend that the first opportunity will be taken of utilising them, providing that such occupation is consistent with the general scheme of distribution, and the necessity for economy.

HC Deb 30 March 1908 vol. 187 cc81-2 81

On the morning of 16 December, the barracks contained elements of the 14th King's Hussars. The men were quickly mustered, issued rifles and twenty rounds each and told to prepare for invasion. Occupying the many trenches that had been dug across the cliff top, they had an excellent view of the bombardment, and, whilst it is unlikely the facility was a primary target, it did receive slight attention as *Derfflinger* and *von der Tann* headed north. *Scarborough Evening News* reported the following:

> A shell burst in the Barracks, Burniston road, but did little damage beyond chipping some of the walls of the buildings. Several burst in the fields between the Barracks and the cliff edge.
>
> 17 December 1914

Later, Admiral Reinhard Scheer wrote, 'The *Derfflinger* also bombarded trenches and barracks at Scarborough.'

So, it would appear Burniston Barracks was also considered a military installation along with two wireless stations at Scarborough, one at Whitby and the batteries at Hartlepool.

Other reasons for choosing the towns on the East Coast are easier to recognise. Since the beginning of the war, an extensive minefield had been developing along the English coast. Mines sown by one side were often augmented by the other; indeed, the raid on Yarmouth had seen many German mines laid. These, once the extent had been worked

Burniston Barracks. The site to the north of the town centre was built in 1861 and served until 1906 as a repository and training base for the Royal Artillery.

out, were added to by the Royal Navy, becoming known as the Southwold minefield. To the north of Whitby, two German minelayers, the *Albatross* and *Nautilus* had, on the night of 25/26 August, laid an extensive field they thought was off the Humber and Tyne. It turned out they were nowhere near their reported positions and subsequently two danger areas were declared – these are important. The northern danger area extended from the Farn Islands south to the River Tees; the southern danger area extended south from Flamborough Head to the River Humber, both fields were 30 miles deep. This left a clear corridor approximately 25 miles wide between Whitby and Filey. This was clearly the easiest route in for Hipper.

The final major reason for the bombardment was the opportunity to carry out Tirpitz' risk theory. With the destruction of the German East Asia Squadron, Berlin recognised that the Grand Fleet was at its weakest. It would take a few weeks to bring it up to battleship strength, and until then, Jellicoe's forces were light a number of important assets. If the German operation could entice out of port a light Royal Naval force, the waiting battleship screen might be able to cause considerable damage. Unfortunately, it was not 1900. The naval map of the world had changed considerably. Russia had not recovered from its ill-fated eastern adventure, France was now actively fighting on the same side as Britain, and assets from the Mediterranean countries were in no position to mount operations in the North Sea. The best the Imperial Navy could hope for was a decisive victory that might force London to reconsider its position. As it turned out, the weather put paid to that. The intended destroyer screen and submarine curtain were abandoned due to the storm on the night of 15 December. That dictated that only the six ships of the 1st Scouting Division and *Kolberg* actually reached the coast. Naturally, the orders were by now to shell the objectives, lay the mines and make it back to the rendezvous point.

Of course, whatever the objectives set for the operation, the outcome was nothing short of a disaster. True, the attacking force suffered very little damage – indeed, the weather caused more to the majority of the vast flotilla than any engagement off the coast of Hartlepool – but what little reputation Germany still had in the United Kingdom simply evaporated over night. By the following day, the national press had taken up the cause. 'German Ghouls Gloating over Murder of English Schoolboys' proclaimed the strap line of *The Daily Mirror*, followed up with 'Berlin's Satisfaction with "Gallant" Fleet that can Kill Civilians' and 'The Wanton War on Women and Children'. *The Daily Sketch* followed with similar sentiment proclaiming 'German "Kultur" means shells on Churches'; the *Scarborough Pictorial*, published 23 December, described the damaged buildings as 'Monuments to Kultur'.

Naturally more vocal, the First Sea Lord wrote to Scarborough Mayor expressing his clear disgust at the unprovoked attack on a defenceless population.

Their hate is a measure of their fear. Its senseless expression is a proof of their impotence and the seed of their dishonour. Whatever feats of arms the German navy may hereafter perform, the stigma of the 'baby killers' of Scarborough will brand its officers and men while sailors sail the sea, believe me dear Mr Mayor.

First Sea Lord of the Admiralty, Winston Churchill

Sunday 20 December 1914

The press had a field day. This cover of a souvenir booklet published by the *Scarborough Mercury* nicely captures the national mood.

The Mayor, Alderman C. C. Graham, replied with typical Churchillian sentiment, closing by declaring,

> As their commanders get older in the service, they will find that an Iron Cross pinned on their chest even by King Herod, will not shield them from the shafts of shame and dishonour.
>
> Mayor of Scarborough, Alderman C. C. Graham
> Monday 21 December 1914

The King sent a message to the town that was to appear in a number of souvenirs printed by E. T. W. Dennis & Sons a few weeks later.

> The people of Scarborough and Whitby have been much in my thoughts during the last week, and I deeply sympathise with the bereaved families in their distress. Please let me know as to the condition of the wounded. I trust they may have a speedy recovery.
>
> George, R.I.

Even the Institute of Certified Grocers felt a letter of support to their Scarborough members:

> We trust however that no personal injury was inflicted on yourself or on any of your immediate friends: and we trust that your property was undamaged.
>
> Saturday 19 December 1914

During his research for *Bombardment: The Day the East Coast Bled*, historian Mark Marsay uncovered a number of replies from Scarborough's grocer fraternity, unfortunately unassigned; however, one extract is worth repeating here:

> As you may think, trade was not brisk during the bombardment, but one of my customers, having fallen short of bacon for breakfast, came in for a pound in

slices during the height of the affair. I have never cut bacon under such irritating circumstances. 'Business as usual' is all very well, but there are limits!

However, it was the editorial that appeared in *The War Illustrated* that is most telling of the direction the bombardment was about to take the nation:

The sequel to Admiral Sturdee's crushing blow arrived with dramatic suddenness. On the 16th inst., after several months of comparative inactivity at Kiel, part of the German Navy visited the East Coast – not, however, to attack a point of any military significance, but to shell the undefended towns of Hartlepool, Scarborough and Whitby. The total loss of life, unfortunately, amounted to eighty-one persons, and many more were wounded. The object of the raid is open to conjecture. If to avenge Von Spee by killing innocent civilians, it is typical of German desperation and cowardice.

Whatever may be the outcome of this raid, this country's foretaste of the horrors of war as waged by the Kaiser's uniformed serfs in bombarding open towns is very timely. It should be the greatest stimulus to recruiting and the required incentive for John Bull at home to see that the doom of the despicable Prussian is swift and sure. The last important attack on our shores took place as long ago as 1667, when De Ruyter, commanding the Dutch Fleet, raided the Thames and Sheerness.

The War Illustrated, 26 December 1914

And join they did. It wasn't long before posters were appearing shouting 'Avenge Scarborough – Up and At Em Now!' Of all the posters produced, the one depicting Britannia leading the men of England forward whilst Scarborough burns in the background is the most famous. Using the simple strap line 'Remember Scarborough! Enlist Now', it is difficult to estimate the actual numbers of recruits the bombardment generated. The War Department claimed that, for every poster, one thousand men joined up; the problem is we do not know the print run!

Regardless of the effectiveness of the posters, the bombardment made the country realise that the war was not going to be over before Christmas and that it would need to consider a new type of struggle, this time on the Home Front. Interestingly, the bombardment appears to have forced the government into mobilising potentially half the population. The Women's Volunteer Reserve (WVR) was formed as a direct response to the bombardment. The organisation had two initial aims: to free up men for service and to organise succour for those left helpless in the community. The WVS also transported the wounded, ran canteens, offered first aid and carried out motoring duties. Interestingly, as an act of solidarity (which was not without its critics), they also wore khaki uniforms and drilled.

So, is it possible to answer the question I asked at the start of this work? Was the bombardment merely an ill-conceived attack on three towns possibly in revenge for the losses inflicted at the Battle of the Falklands? The simple answer is no. The road to the bombardment falls into a number of categories but can be simplified into two main themes.

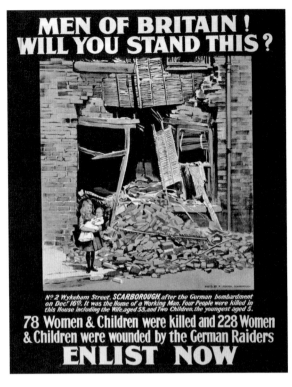

This page: The bombardment was a godsend for the government. The myth of the 'baby killers' prevailed throughout. Claims were that each poster raised 1,000 men.

The territorial aspirations of the recently formed German nation were a century behind other European nations. Traditionally, Continental Europe was dominated by large armies; territorial expansion required a strong navy. The events off the coast of South Africa allowed Alfred von Tirpitz to argue strongly for a larger, more effective navy, possibly one that could rival the Royal Navy. The appointment of John Fisher as First Sea Lord allowed for the modernisation of the Royal Navy; however, it also made it possible for other nations to compete in an arms race where only manufacturing capability would eventually produce a winner. Tirpitz, realising it was unlikely that Germany would be able to confront Britain at sea alone, devised the risk theory. Whist the Royal Navy is spread across the globe, it is weak at home. If damage could be done in the North Sea, another country could take advantage of the situation, effectively removing Britain from the top of the seafaring nations. By the outbreak of the First World War, risk was unlikely to succeed, as the only other credible fleets were either allied with Britain or had already been lost, primarily in the East. Nevertheless, when news of the losses off the Falklands reached Germany, the Imperial Navy High Command realised this was their chance and undertook a risk-based operation. Even if no third party was forthcoming, enough damage might be done to alter Britain's attitude to a war on the Continent.

The selection of Scarborough, Whitby and Hartlepool as targets is multifaceted. Location made the towns vulnerable to attack, especially since Scarborough and Whitby faced the 25-mile gap in the minefields. As to their military worth, all three had assets both sides were already destroying around the world, the most obvious being the wireless stations. This up-and-coming device had already revolutionised naval warfare and both sides clearly felt bombardment of such facilities was justified. Hartlepool is easier to explain, as it had manned coastal batteries and elements of the Floating Coastal Defence. It was the belief that Scarborough also had coastal defences that sealed that town's fate. What strengthens the German argument rests in two areas. Firstly, Scarborough had a long and presumably well-known association with coastal artillery, especially since Burniston Barracks had been specifically constructed with artillery in mind. Second, the year before the bombardment, a German visit had been specifically shown around the castle and other buildings on the headland. Mention was probably made of its defensive aspects and the role it once played in defending the coast against invaders. Subsequently, when the gunners on *Derfflinger* and *von der Tann, Moltke, Blücher* and *Seydlitz* sighted their targets and let loose, they probably did it with all conviction that they were right in what they were doing.

Of course, all this pales into insignificance when considered within the bigger picture. Millions were to die across the world as the twentieth century was punctuated by conflict, due, in part, to the naval arms race sparked in 1905 by Fisher's Dreadnought and Germany's intention to expand. I'm sure this will not be the last word on the subject – indeed, issues surrounding civilian casualties are often contentious – however, I am convinced that we should consider the bombardment the product of a series of events. Events that were sometimes subtle, sometimes global in size, but events that would shape certainly the First World War, but probably the whole of the twentieth century if we were to look hard enough.

Bibliography

Corbett, J. S., *Naval Operations: History of the Great War Based on Official Documents, Volume Two* (Naval and Military Press Ltd, Imperial War Museum, 2nd ed., 1929)

Halpern, P. G., *A Naval History of World War I* (Routledge, London, 2003 ed.)

Hartington-Jones, J., *The German Attack on Scarborough: December 16 1914* (Quoin Publishing, Huddersfield, 1989)

Marsay, M., *Bombardment: The Day the East Coast Bled* (Great Northern Publishing, Scarborough, 1999)

Massie, K. R., *Dreadnought: Britain, Germany and the Coming of the Great War* (Random House, New York, 1991)

Miller, F., *Under Shell-Fire: The Hartlepools Scarborough & Whitby under German Shell-Fire* (Robert Martin Ltd., West Hartlepool, 2nd ed. 1915)

Mould, D., *Remember Scarborough 1914!* (Hendon Publishing Co. Ltd, Nelson, 1978)

Pitt, B., *Coronel and Falkland: Two Great Naval Battles of the First World War* (Cassell, London, 1960)

Scarborough Mercury Co. Ltd. *A German Crime: Bombardment of Scarborough, December 16th 1914* (Scarborough, 1914/5)

Government Papers and Hansard are through Parliamentary Licence No. P20080000286 28/09/2008 – 27/09/2013.